LORDSHIP
AND
DISCIPLESHIP

STUDIES IN BIBLICAL THEOLOGY

LORDSHIP
AND
DISCIPLESHIP

EDUARD SCHWEIZER

ALEC R. ALLENSON, INC.
635 EAST OGDEN AVENUE
NAPERVILLE, ILL.

First English edition 1960

© SCM Press Ltd 1960
Translated from the German
ERNIEDRIGUNG UND ERHÖHUNG BEI JESUS
UND SEINEN NACHFOLGERN
(Zwingli-Verlag, Zürich, 1955)
with revisions by the author

To
COLGATE ROCHESTER DIVINITY SCHOOL
its warm fellowship, its free atmosphere,
its sincere scholarship,
its natural piety

Printed in Great Britain by
W. & J. Mackay & Co Ltd, Chatham

CONTENTS

PREFACE

THE Church to which we are privileged to preach Jesus Christ is not greatly troubled by a sense of sin, as was the ancient Palestinian Church or the Church of Luther's day. Like the Hellenistic Church, however, she is troubled by the question of the meaning of man's life and by fear of a fate against which man is helpless. If one thinks that it is not permissible, in the first place, by all possible psychological means, to arouse a sense of sin, in order that one's answer will be welcome, then one must ask whether the NT supplies an answer to these very questions. Beginning therefore with the confessions of Christ influenced by Hellenism, I have directed my inquiries back to the message of the Palestinian Church and of Jesus himself. Perhaps modern man first encounters him who calls him to follow him, who thereby becomes his 'Lord', and who thus delivers him from fear and meaninglessness, in order to understand that he is the One who was crucified 'for him'. I am convinced that this 'for him' is the centre of the message. We see nowadays, however, how the same message became relevant to the Jewish Church as an answer to questions quite different from those confronting the Hellenistic Church, indeed that even within these groups a lively discussion took place of which we find the marks in the NT. Thus an attempt like this may perhaps help the preaching of the Gospel to remain a *viva vox* and not deteriorate into a gramophone record.

This book is an entirely revised edition of my work, *Erniedrigung und Erhöhung bei Jesus und seinen Nachfolgern* (Zwingli-Verlag, Zürich, 1955, *Abhandlungen zur Theologie des alten und neuen Testaments*, ed. W. Eichrodt and O. Cullmann, no. 28). On the one hand I have drawn the lines much wider and in particular given considerably more attention to Paul; on the other hand I have to a great extent left out the discussion, with the literature on the subject, particularly concerning disputed exegetical questions and

7

the treatment of Hellenism, and given only the most indispensable references. For more thorough scholarly discussion I must therefore once and for all refer to the German edition.

The chapters of the two editions correspond as follows:

English edition	German edition
1	1
2	5
3	6a–e, 7a–c
4	6c, 10, 8
5	9, 12b–c
6	11, 6h, 7c
7	6f–g, 16i–k, 7e, d, 12f, i
8	6i, 7h, 6k–l, 7f–g
9	2–4, 16p–q
10	121, 13
11	7i–l, 16e–h, l–o, 17
12	15, 16a–d
13	—
14	14

Zürich,
25 August 1956   EDUARD SCHWEIZER

ACKNOWLEDGEMENTS

I dedicate this my first book in English to Colgate Rochester Divinity School, where our family is spending a most happy term owing to the fatherly kindness of its president, W. E. Saunders, and the friendly assistance of the whole faculty and staff, especially the librarians.

Rochester, New York
11 November 1959   EDUARD SCHWEIZER

ABBREVIATIONS

Bull. J.Ryl.L.	Bulletin of the John Rylands Library
Corp. Herm.	Corpus Hermeticum, ed. Nock, Paris, since 1945
EvTh	Evangelische Theologie
Exp. Times	Expository Times
Handbuch	*Handbuch zum neuen Testament*, ed. H. Lietzmann
Harvard Th.R.	Harvard Theological Review
JBL	Journal of Biblical Literature
JThSt	Journal of Theological Studies
Meyer	*Kritisch-exegetischer Kommentar über das NT*, ed. H. A. W. Meyer
N.T.St.	New Testament Studies
Orph. fra.	Orphicorum fragmenta, ed. O. Kern, 1922
I QS	Qumran Manuscripts, Manual of Discipline
R. Biblique	Revue Biblique
R.G.G.	*Die Religion in Geschichte und Gegenwart,* 3rd Ed. (ed. K. Galling)
SAH	Sitzungsberichte der Heidelberger Akademie der Wissenschaften, phil-hist. Abt.
SJT	Scottish Journal of Theology
Str-B.	*Kommentar zum NT aus Talmud und Midrasch,* ed. H. L. Strack und P. Billerbeck
ThLZ	Theologische Literaturzeitung
Th.Wb.	*Theologisches Wörterbuch zum NT*, ed. G. Kittel
ThZ	Theologische Zeitschrift, Basel.
VuF	Verkündigung und Forschung
ZAW	Zeitschrift für die alttestamentliche Wissenschaft
ZNW	Zeitschrift für die neutestamentliche Wissenschaft
ZRGG	Zeitschrift für die Religions-und Geistesgeschichte
ZThK	Zeitschrift für Theologie und Kirche

I

FOLLOWING JESUS[1]

WHEN in a valley in the mountains there is a sudden heavy fall of snow, a child visiting his grandmother may not be able to reach home again. But when father comes home from his work he will fetch him, lead the way and with his strong shoulders make a way through the snowdrifts. The child follows, step by step, in the footsteps of father, and yet in an entirely different manner. If the father wanted to be just an 'example' to the child, then the child would have to make his own way ten yards away from the father and merely imitate the manner in which the latter makes his way. If the father wanted to act 'vicariously' for the child, in the strict sense of the word, then the child would stay with grandmother and think: Father is going home in my stead.

This example *cannot* have the intention of emphasizing that the child 'too must do something'. He certainly does do something, and something very concrete at that. He follows a road on which there is sunshine and cold wind, soft snow and hard ice. But what he is doing is a matter of course. He is going home just as he went home yesterday, and he is pleased to go home. But this is certainly true: that he is involved in what father is doing, involved 'after the event', but yet involved step by step; so much so that he learns to see what father is doing before his eyes and step by step practises what he sees.

This example may stand at the beginning of our investigation. It is not meant to be a solution, it could not be that because it is just a picture. But it raises the *question* for the NT whether early Christianity has not regarded Jesus Christ as in the same sense 'going on before' and, if so, what this meant to those who so understood him. There can be no doubt about the fact that Jesus

[1]German *Nachfolge* is usually translated as 'imitation' which is always inaccurate and very often impossible, as is the case here. In the present book it has been translated as 'following' or 'discipleship'.

called disciples to follow him.[1] The word 'follow' in its new specific meaning has a firm place in the tradition.[2] In the NT we find only the verb which, with the sole exception of Rev. 14.4, is used exclusively of the relationship to the earthly Jesus. This shows how realistically concrete this whole concept of following Christ was to the Church.

The Greek world already used the expression in a figurative sense. When the Greeks speak of 'following' in connexion with a deity they mean that man should become like the deity. In Stoic philosophy Nature is substituted for the deity. But there too the ideal is to become conformable to Nature by harmoniously adapting oneself to it. In Judaism two lines of development can be traced. The word is used in the first place of concrete following in the literal sense of the word. The OT uses it especially of those who 'follow Baal', that is to say, who forsake Jahveh, and this is why it is avoided in connexion with true religion. But the word clearly contains the notion that such following is the act of a servant who belongs to his lord (*baal*). The same view persists in Rabbinical literature, where the expression denotes the act of the disciples who walk at a respectful distance behind their master. But beside this another view arises in Rabbinical literature which certainly cannot be accounted for without the influence of the Greek meaning of the term. As it is obviously impossible literally to follow God, to walk in his footsteps, the Rabbis declare: 'This means rather: to follow the *virtues* of God'. The concept thereby describes the *imitation* of God, as in the Greek world, with this qualification that in Judaism ethical effort, understood as obedience to the Law, has a more central place. The fact that the expression 'following God' is not found in the NT shows that we have to take our lead from the first and not from the second line of development.

Mark 1.17 f. presents the calling in its simplest structure. 'And Jesus said unto them, Come ye after me, and I will make you to

---

[1] Cf. G. Wingren, *ThLZ* 1950, p. 385 ff. and especially Gerhard Kittel, *Theologisches Wörterbuch zum neuen Testament*, Stuttgart, since 1932, I, p. 210 ff. How important |the call of Jesus was is shown by the fact that μαθητεύειν is constantly used as a transitive verb (K. H. Rengstorf, ibid., IV, p. 465).

[2] It is to be found in Mark, in the tradition common to Matthew and Luke which we call here Q without discussing its supposed form, and in John.

become fishers of men. And straightway they left the nets, and followed him.' Three points appear to be of interest: 1. The call comes from Jesus. That is the beginning of it all. 2. It is a call to service,[1] and Jesus himself creates the possibility of such service. 3. Obedience entails forsaking old ties. Mark 1.20 has a similar structure. The second point is not expressly mentioned. With regard to the third point it is made clear that it is a question not only of giving up one's occupation but also one's family.

The next passage is Mark 2.14: 'And as he passed by, he saw Levi the son of Alphaeus sitting at the place of toll, and he saith unto him, Follow me. And he arose and followed him.' The word must first of all be considered independently of the following story, as the connexion between the two is probably not original. Again it is emphasized that everything proceeds from Jesus' calling. Again it is emphasized that following Jesus entails a break with other ties. But far more essential is the fact that this time it is a *publican* who is called, a man outside the bounds of the worshipping community of God's people. This lends to the call the character of an act of grace. Thereby God breaks through the barrier which hitherto had been considered insurmountable. It is precisely the unclean, the disobedient, the sinner who is called in this case. That this is not overemphasizing the point is shown by the tradition. Jesus is continually being reproached for his association with sinners. What according to Deut. 21.20 the parents of a stubborn and rebellious son have to say to the elders of the city before the latter stone him to death: 'This our son . . . is a riotous liver and a drunkard', that the people say of Jesus: 'Behold a gluttonous man and a wine-bibber, a friend of publicans and sinners!' (Matt. 11.19). They are the people with whom he associates (Mark 2.14, 15 ff.; Luke 15.1; 19.1 ff.). He promises the Kingdom of God to them first of all (Matt. 21.31; Luke 18.10 ff.). They before all others have allowed themselves to be called to repentance (Matt. 21.32; Luke 3.12; 7.29). Mark emphasizes this in particular when he links the story of the meal with publicans with this calling of Levi.

The very fact that Jesus calls people to follow him, and that he

---

[1]In Mark 15.41 (=Matt. 27.55, cf. Luke 8.2 f.), also, ἀκολουθεῖν is interpreted as διακονεῖν.

does this with the consequence that they leave boat and toll-office and family, denotes a quite astonishing knowledge of his mission. Nothing like this is to be found except in connexion with the would-be messiahs, Judas and Theudas, and with John the Baptist, who was however regarded by his disciples as a messianic figure. This holds good to an even greater extent of the breaking through all barriers as in the case of Levi. Grace becomes an event in such calling. The question whether or not Jesus himself expressly promised the forgiveness of sin is far less relevant than the fact that by his actions he has brought the forgiveness of sin as an actual event. By his calling Levi to himself, by his sitting down to a meal with publicans these *have been* adopted into fellowship with God.

Whether the tradition of the following words goes back to genuine sayings of Jesus is not quite so sure. First of all Mark 10.21: 'And Jesus looking upon him loved him, and said unto him, One thing thou lackest: go, sell whatsoever thou hast, and give to the poor, and thou shalt have treasure in heaven; and come, follow me.' Here too the first emphasis is on Jesus' calling. His action is underlined by his looking the questioner in the eye and loving him. In the passages discussed so far it was always said that Jesus 'saw' the man; but here this is described as a conscious act. If one recognizes that in all the analogous cases so far the call to follow was the decisive call, which as a matter of course entailed the forsaking of any ties which might prove a hindrance, then there is no room for a different interpretation here. The great discussion as to whether this passage teaches a law universally applicable, or a double morality, may be regarded as not to the point. The only point to be observed is that the 'righteous' is called as well as the 'sinner', and that both have their ties which have to be severed. But 'the most astonishing aspect of this amazing story'[1] is in the fact that following Jesus is more than the fulfilment of all the commandments. Even voluntary poverty is merely a means to this end.[2]

In Mark 10.28 f. Peter declares: 'Lo, we have left all, and have

[1]E. Lohmeyer, *Das Evangelium des Markus (Meyer)*, Göttingen, 1937, p. 212.
[2]W. Zimmerli discusses this story on the background of the Old Testament pattern, in which the believer questions the priest about the 'life' that he is longing for. He thinks that it could depict an historical event in the earthly life of Jesus (*EvTh* 1959, p. 90 ff.)

followed thee' and Jesus replies that everyone who in this way leaves all that he has will receive hundredfold reward. Here too it should be kept in mind first of all that following Jesus entails severing the old ties.[1] In contrast to the previous occasions there is no mention here of specific things. The absoluteness of this severance is underlined: they have left 'all'. It becomes very evident here that following Jesus means self-denial, humility, poverty, suffering and that it is undertaken in view of the promised reward, though it is made quite clear that this reward is dependent on Jesus' promise, that it is beyond any merit, and that therefore it cannot be claimed by the disciple. Herein we find a continuation of the Jewish knowledge, as expressed in the OT, of the righteous man's way through humiliation, poverty and suffering to the promised gracious raising up by God.

Mark 10.32 is not quite clear in this respect. The verse is introducing a section which the evangelist sets off by means of the expression 'in the way' appearing at its beginning as well as at its end (10.32, 52). The significance of this way of Jesus to Jerusalem is stressed by the whole of v. 32. For nowhere else is Jesus said to lead the way, except in the prophecy 14.28 = 16.7. He is here the master going before his disciples who have to follow him.[2] Moreover the importance of this way is marked by the amazement of the crowd and by the fear of those who follow him.[3] Out of these Jesus takes the twelve aside to explain to them his way of suffering and humiliation. Thus it seems that the term 'follow' is used as elsewhere in the pregnant sense of participation in Jesus'

[1]This is described by the aorist tense as an act once and for all, while following is described by a perfect tense as an action which one has resolved to do but which is continuing. This also demonstrates that the latter is the decisive act to which the severance of ties is merely meant to be a preliminary.

[2]The same is expressed by the changing tenses in vv. 38 (Jesus' way of suffering *has* already begun) and 39 (the disciples *will* share in it).

[3]The group following him is clearly distinguished from the other one which is amazed. It is true that at the end of the preceding passage the disciples were the centre of the interest. One would therefore think that they were the amazed ones. But 4.21, 24, 34–36 (cf. with 4.10, 11, 13) show how easily Mark changes the meaning of 'they', referring first to the disciples, then, without any indication of a change, to the crowd. It seems therefore more probable that 'following' is to be understood as in 10.28, 52 and very often, as describing those who at least have taken some interest in Jesus' preaching or even decided to be his disciples; whereas the group of amazed ones are mere lookers-on.

vocation to suffering and death.[1] This is supported by the following passage (10.35–45) which makes it clear that his disciples must share in their master's way, and by the last section (10.46–52) where the healed blind man, saved by his 'faith' and 'following Jesus in the way', is a symbol for every one whose eyes are opened by the grace of God so that they may believe and follow Jesus in his way of humiliation.[2]

This last aspect appears in an emphasized form in a word which we find in the 'Logia-source' Q on which both Matthew and Luke are based (Matt. 8.19 f.–Luke 9.57 f.) where to a man who wants to 'follow thee, whithersoever thou goest', Jesus replies: 'The foxes have holes, and the birds of heaven have nests; but the Son of man hath not where to lay his head.' This saying could be very old and probably dates back to Jesus himself.[3]

The words Matt. 8.22–Luke 9.60, in both cases connected with this 'Follow me, and leave the dead to bury their own dead', underline almost more heavily than any other saying the absoluteness with which discipleship excludes all other ties. The same note is struck by the saying, only found in Luke, about the man who has put his hand to the plough and must not look back. Here too the following of Jesus is still understood in a very concrete way. Luke tells how Jesus, after having been rejected by the Samaritans, goes to another village. Matthew says that he is planning a

---

[1] Lohmeyer, *Markus*, p. 220; Vincent Taylor, *The Gospel according to St Mark*, London, 1953, p. 437 ff.

[2] In the same way the admonition to take up one's cross (8.34 ff.) follows the prediction of his suffering (8.31; cf. also 9.35 after 9.31). The misunderstanding in 10.35–37 corresponds to the misunderstanding of Peter (8.32 f.; cf. the dispute about greatness 9.33–37 after the second prophecy of the passion), the symbolic healing of the blind man in 10.46–52 to that in 8.22–26 (cf. the healing and the discussion about faith in 9.23 ff.) and the triumphant entry into Jerusalem (11.1–10) to the transfiguration (9.2–8).

[3] Arguments are given by W. G. Kümmel, *Verheissung und Erfüllung*, Zürich, 1953, p. 40, Engl. tr. *Promise and Fulfilment* by D. M. Barton, London, 1957, p. 46. The suggestion that here we have a word that at first simply spoke of man ('son of man' in Aramaic!) in general and was not applied to *the* Son of man, Jesus, until later is untenable. For this could certainly not be regarded as a proverb of general application, but at the utmost as a word referring to quite specific conditions of war, which however did not occur in or near Palestine at the time when this word is supposed to have been current. G. Bornkamm (in *The Background of the New Testament and its Eschatology*, ed. W. D. Davies and D. Daube, Cambridge, 1956, p. 239) shows how Matt. 8.23–26) has modified an old miracle story into a treatise on the Church following Jesus. Cf. p. 78 here.

crossing to the eastern shore of the Lake.[1] But Jesus' reply in itself, independent of the context in which we now find the saying, shows that the reference is to a concrete going-together-with-someone, in which the follower, the disciple, shares in the privations and in the rejection of his Master. Whosoever wants to follow Jesus must be prepared to share his fate. But this means: to be without security and a home.

It is clear in all three sayings that discipleship brings no visible advantages, but entails self-denial and privation, the first word expressly implying that the disciple shares the fate of his Master.

Extremely relevant is the section Mark 8.31 ff. We start from v. 34: 'If any man would come after me, let him deny himself, and take up his cross, and follow me.'[2] This saying is also found in Q, and reads in Matt. 10.38 (par. Luke 14.27): 'He that doth not take his cross and follow after me, is not worthy of me.' Being the shorter form the latter seems to be original. If so, then Mark was the first to interpret 'taking up the cross' as 'self-denial'. Then this saying could not with certainty be attributed to Jesus. Crucifixion, it is true, was the most general form of execution, and it is by no means impossible that Jesus, when he wanted to give a vivid description of the man who had completely finished with his life and had buried all his own expectations, desires and designs, made use of this picture. Nevertheless we know of no real parallels.[3] Of course it is true that Jesus made this demand, but how far he did this in general terms, apart from concrete demands, one cannot be sure.

Connected with this logion is the second: 'For whosoever would save his life shall lose it; and whosoever shall lose his life for my sake and the gospel's shall save it.'[4] This saying has been

---

[1] Cf. p. 16, 3, and p. 78.

[2] For the history of this word, cf. E. Dinkler in 'Neutestamentliche Studien für Rudolf Bultmann' (Beihefte *ZNW*, 21) Berlin, 1954, p. 110 ff.

[3] The rabbinic parallel in *Str-B.* I, p. 587 is called forth by the picture of Isaac carrying the wood on his shoulder, and is of uncertain date. But in Hellenistic stories the carrying of a cross is regarded as a disgrace (E. Percy, *Die Botschaft Jesu*, 1953, p. 172). It is possible that Jesus had spoken merely of self-denial, that the Church had given this a more 'Christian' appearance by speaking of taking up the cross, and that eventually Q had only the more 'devotional' term left.

[4] The connexion with the preceding sentence is not absolutely certain. The two sentences, it is true, are also connected in Matthew's version of Q

handed down in various forms and, except for the clause 'for the gospel's', which is found only in Mark, and makes the saying universally applicable beyond the time of the earthly Jesus, it may well be attributed to Jesus. This shows firstly that the entire tradition has interpreted the saying on bearing the cross to mean readiness to set oneself free from all ties, even from that of one's own life; and, secondly, that Jesus himself has probably formulated in a universally applicable way what he was doing by every call to discipleship. Even if the words 'for my sake' did not originally belong to this phrase, there could be no possible doubt but that on the lips of Jesus it signifies the man who listens to him and walks in a new way for the sake of his calling, so that the only remaining question is whether the emphasis was on obedience to his word or to his person. He is promised self-denial and suffering, perhaps even death.

Mark 8.36 f. is of doubtful origin. The words may originate in a profane proverb. They are of no consequence in this connexion.

On the other hand Mark 8.38 (Matt. 10.33) might easily be a saying of Jesus, probably in its shorter form, Luke 9.26. This conclusion can be drawn from the unusual stylistic distinction between 'I' and 'the Son of man' which probably with conscious restraint seeks to indicate that he who is speaking is the One who is appointed to be exalted and to bear witness in the Last Judgment.[1] That is to say that a man's present attitude towards Jesus determines his fate at the Last Judgment. The negative form may be original, but there is, of course, no doubt that Jesus has also spoken positively of what awaits his disciples, even though he avoids all apocalyptic pictures.[2] He has spoken of reward, but always in such a manner that this is not reckoned according to

---

(ch. 10.38 f.) but in Luke (14.27; 17.33) they are separated. According to Matt. 10.37, however, the word on taking up the cross was preceded in Q by 'He that loveth father and mother more than me. . . .' In Luke 14.26 this appears in the form '. . . hateth not . . . yea his own life, he cannot be my disciple'. Having already mentioned the demand that one should hate one's own life, Luke could dispense with the other saying here and make use of it in ch. 17.33, where perhaps he already found it in the tradition in a slightly different form.

[1] Cf. p. 39 ff.
[2] Cf. the saying Mark 10.29 f. discussed above; also Matt. 19.28; Luke 22.29 f.

merit, because the only important thing is the faithfulness of the disciple.

In the Synoptic Gospels this series of logia is linked with the first announcement of the Passion, Mark 8.31–33. It remains doubtful whether this connexion can be attributed to Jesus. In Q most of the words occur in a different context, and Mark 8.34a forms a new introduction.[1] Moreover Mark 8.31 belongs to the stereotyped announcements of the passion, which are very doubtful historically. But it is in every respect probable that Jesus has consciously and emphatically spoken of his being rejected by men, as expressed by some logia in a very primitive form.[2] The scene near Caesarea Philippi is almost unthinkable without such an announcement. Mark undoubtedly presents the oldest form. According to him Jesus neither welcomes nor rejects Peter's confession, but adopts a very reserved attitude and forbids his disciples to speak about it. This picture is nonsensical without some positive conclusion which can only be a prediction of his passion.[3]

[1]Though perhaps merely to emphasize its universal application.

[2]Luke 17.25: 'But first must he suffer many things and be rejected of this generation.' Mark 9.12: 'How is it written of the Son of man, that he should suffer many things and be set at naught?' Also Luke 12.50; 13.33 and 24.7. Noteworthy is Luke 9.44: 'The Son of man shall be delivered up into the hands of men,' because Mark here has a long announcement of the passion and Luke's language shows a clumsy Semitism.

[3]The case is different if one regards this whole section as unhistorical (as does Percy, *Die Botschaft Jesu*, p. 227 ff., in spite of his rejection of Bultmann). This seems to me almost impossible. In the Marcan form, where Jesus rejects rather than accepts the name of Messiah, it cannot be a transformed Easter narrative or a creation of the later Church. One would then have to regard the form in Matthew as the older one (R. Bultmann, *Die Geschichte der synoptischen Tradition*, Göttingen, 1931, p. 275 ff.). But who could believe that Mark 8.33 is a creation of the Evangelist and that the word to Peter, Matt. 16.17–19 was cut out by him? One could hardly suspect him of anti-Petrine bias (16.7; cf. 3.16; 5.37; 9.2; 11.21; 13.3); and it is highly improbable that Peter was ever an exponent of Judaistic Christianity (O. Cullmann, *Petrus, Jünger—Apostel—Märtyrer*, Zürich, 1952, pp. 39 ff. Eng. ed. translated by Floyd V. Filson, pp. 42 ff.). Geographical references are not always a sign of good tradition, but one so unexpected as Caesarea Philippi certainly is. Of course, v. 27a could be connected with v. 26 (the place-name is absent from Luke); but what would be the sense at the end of a section? It is admirably suited to our section because, according to Rabbinic literature, the 'upper tower above Caesarea Philippi' is the boundary between the Holy Land and the country outside (A. Schlatter, *Der Evangelist Matthäus*, Stuttgart, 1929, p. 502). If the sharp word to Peter cannot have been invented by the early

Looking back on the words of Jesus on discipleship, on following him, some points become clear:

1. Jesus has called men to follow him; this allegiance to his person he regards as a decisive, indeed as *the* decisive act.

2. His calling is the beginning of something new, changing all things. It takes place in sovereign liberty and can at once assume the character of an act of divine grace.

3. Following Jesus means togetherness with Jesus and service to him.

4. It entails giving up all other ties, to boat and tax-office, to father and mother, in short, to one's own life, to oneself.

5. As Jesus' own way, by divine necessity, leads to rejection, suffering and death, and only so to glory, so also the way of those who follow him.

This holds good even if we cannot be sure that *all* the words under review can be attributed to Jesus. But it will be very difficult to find an answer to the question, whether this call was directed only to a particular group within the number of those who were obedient to Jesus. On one occasion, Mark 9.38, explicit reference is made to a man who 'does not follow Jesus' and is yet recognized by him. Moreover it is evident that Jesus by no means called all those who wanted to obey him to that outward discipleship which implied the abandoning of family and occupation.[1] Following Jesus, therefore, is not a new method of attaining salvation, an ascetic road to salvation.[2] In another sense however the call is addressed to all. Words like those on hating one's own life may not have been made universally applicable for the first time by the Church, but may have been uttered by Jesus in this universal sense. So far the answer to the call of Jesus does imply the decision of the Last Judgment over life and death.

Church, then Peter must somehow have attempted to keep Jesus from his journey to Jerusalem. Then Jesus must have pointed out before the event that he intended to suffer. No place is more likely for this than Caesarea Philippi where the decision had to be made whether he was to remain faithful to the land of Israel or go outside its borders. Cf. also R. P. Casey, in *The Background of the New Testament and its Eschatology*, p. 59.

[1]The man healed in Mark 5.18 ff. is even forbidden to do this. The desire 'that he should be with him' corresponds exactly with the intention at the call of the disciples.

[2]In this respect the fellowship of the disciples differs from the Qumran sect.

Only the disciple can know who Jesus really is. This is the meaning of Mark 8.27 ff. No formula merely taught, and learned and repeated by a disciple can adequately describe this. One cannot know who Jesus is until one shares his way with him. This is the meaning of the 'Messianic secret', this is the explanation of his reserve in connexion with the title of Christ, which is not wrong but which does not apply without qualification; therefore that mysterious speaking of the Son of man, which allows for a quite vague interpretation as well as one of extreme emphasis and in the light of which, therefore, one could regard him as an ordinary man of humble estate, or as the One who has to go through humiliation to exaltation and to fulfil the expectations of late Judaism.[1]

Jesus has also expected that his disciples should be prepared to deny everything, including their lives. Suffering and tribulation govern their future. But such a decision for or against him will determine the decision in the Last Judgment. This is why the disciple who follows Jesus never expected to cease following him and to become a master himself, and to gather disciples round him, as the disciple of a rabbi was wont to do. He has followed Jesus in such a way as one can only follow either Baal or Jahveh, a would-be Messiah or the Messiah. From the very beginning his faith has been such that he has expected complete salvation from Jesus.[2]

---

[1]This also implies the very open character of the group of disciples, which is not separated from the rest of Israel either by a formulated creed or by a new rite or by a new meeting place (as, e.g. Qumran). Cf. E. Schweizer, *Gemeinde und Gemeindeordnung im Neuen Testament* (Zwingli-Verlag, Zürich, 1959, p. 14 ff).

[2]If to an Israelite the 'Covenant' really is an 'agreement to follow' (J. Ellul, *Le fondement théologique du droit*, Neuchâtel, 1948, p. 37 f.) then the Lord's Supper is the actual ratification of this Covenant. The idea of the Covenant, of such central importance also in the Qumran sect, is then the most ancient idea concerning the Lord's Supper, which from the very beginning is connected with the future glory. The Lord's Supper, then, is the pledge given to the disciples of the living presence of their Lord and of the fulfilment of the Covenant which he accomplishes by his very passion and death (cf. E. Schweizer, 'Das Herrenmahl im N.T.', *ThLZ*, 1954, p. 579 ff., and the article 'Abendmahl' in *Die Religion in Geschichte und Gegenwart*, 3rd ed., Tübingen, 1957, I, p. 10 ff.).

II

THE SUFFERING AND EXALTED RIGHTEOUS
ONE IN JUDAISM

A SECOND fact can certainly be established historically: Jesus has
been rejected in Jerusalem and has been put to death with ignom-
iny and suffering. This meant for the time being the end of the
disciples' following. Even if Jesus himself had expected and indeed predicted his death and resurrection, the disciples were quite
unprepared for these events. They fled, probably all the way back
to Galilee. The new beginning was again made entirely by Jesus:
he appeared to them.

Unfortunately we know very little of what followed. It is
certain that the disciples returned to Jerusalem and, together with
their families and very soon also with many new converts, con-
stituted themselves the Israel of the Last Days. I also believe
that this first period was characterized by the experience of the
Spirit, which manifested itself in an enthusiastic form.[1] Prophets
and prophecies have probably been a strong influence in the first
years of the Church. It is possible that for a while the expectation
of the approaching *parousia* suppressed any other questions.[2] But

[1]Luke knows only the names of prophets originating from Judaea (Acts
11.27; 21.9–11). In the OT the pouring out of the Spirit had already been
promised to the Church of the Latter Days. The story in Acts 2.1–21 can
scarcely have arisen without at least some historical origin, and the change in
the attitude of the disciples is plain.

[2]One should take into account the fact that a great deal of Apocalyptic
material was not added to our tradition until later in times full of tension, up
to the 'sixties and 'seventies of the first century. In our texts it is evident that
the idea of the Son of man is closely connected with the *parousia*. His coming
with the clouds may originally have referred to his exaltation (cf. p. 39 and
J. A. T. Robinson, *Jesus and his coming*, London, 1957, pp. 36–58). But even
this meant his appointment as the witness for the Last Judgment. I agree
entirely with Dr Robinson that the expectation of the future and the ethical
exhortation were originally closely linked together and were not separated
until later (cf. Luke 12.57–59; 13.6–9 with Matt. 5.25 f.; 24.32 f., and Robinson, p. 98 f.). But if Jesus expected the impending crisis, and if he spoke of

we must say that this expectation has not exercised any substantial influence on the earliest summaries of the Church's faith. Moreover the fact of Jesus' life and death was already a decisive question for the very early Church which still had a living expectation that the *parousia* was at hand. They were after all to a large extent the same people who had accompanied Jesus, who had witnessed his humiliation and who above all had been completely thrown off their balance through his passion and death. How were they to speak of that time? Of their following him in Galilee? Of his humiliation and execution? And of the miracle of his deliverance from death? Did they have any example at their disposal in the light of which these events could be understood? Was there any instance in contemporary Judaism that could throw light on this strange career of Jesus?

In the OT as well as in later Judaism humility and self-humiliation, or acceptance of humiliation from God's hand, were expected of a pious man and thought to be highly praiseworthy. This is so obvious that we do not need proof. The righteous man is always the man who is lowly, humble, suffering, rejected by the world. Here are a few passages which show that for such a humiliation of the righteous one his exaltation is promised as a reward. 'Jahveh maketh poor, and maketh rich: He bringeth low, he also lifteth up. He raiseth up the poor out of the dust, he lifteth up the needy from the dunghill, To make them sit with princes, And inherit the throne of glory' (I Sam. 2.7 f.). 'He abases the (words of?) pride and sustains him who casts down his eyes' (Job 22.29). 'Those that walk in pride he is able to abase' (Dan.

---

the Judgment, of heaven and earth passing away (Robinson, pp. 37, 59 ff.), then he cannot have been referring *merely* to the fall of Jerusalem. If he did not speak of his second Advent, as it seems to follow from the analysis of the tradition (cf. p. 39), he yet expected that the crisis would lead to the Last Judgment and the coming Kingdom of God (cf. also Luke 22.15–18, 28–30, and the author's article 'Abendmahl' in *R.G.G.*[3], I, pp. 10–21). No doubt Jesus preached the Kingdom of God as something in the future. But in the acts and words of Jesus it becomes present *to the hearer* by his being called to a decision. But even so its advent remains a future event. Indeed there are hardly any genuine words of Jesus which explicitly state that it has already come. Moreover in the old tradition the statements on the Son of man and on the Kingdom of God do not seem to have been connected (Ph. Vielhauer, *Festschrift für G. Dehn*, Neukirchen, 1957, pp. 51–97 but cf. p. 40, n. 2 here!). This explains how the Church, on the OT model, could speak of Jesus' *advent* for judgment as early as the time of I Thess.

4.34). 'A man's pride shall bring him low: But he that is of a lowly spirit shall obtain honour' (Prov. 29.23). 'The greater thou art the more thou shouldst humble thyself, then thou shalt find grace before God' (Ecclus. 3.18). Hillel (*circa* 20 B.C.): 'My humiliation is my exaltation, my exaltation is my humiliation.' Ben Azai (*circa* A.D. 110): 'If thou makest a fool of thyself for the sake of the words of the Law the Law will exalt thee in the end.' Rabbi Joshua ben Levi (*circa* A.D. 250); speaking on the world to come; 'I have seen the world turned upside down, the highest were made lowest and the lowest highest.' Rabbi Tanchumah ben Abba (*circa* A.D. 380): 'If I exalt myself then they will lower my seat . . . and if I humble myself they will raise my seat.'[1] 'Whosoever shall exalt himself shall be humbled; and whosoever shall humble himself shall be exalted' (Matt. 23.12 and par.). 'Humble yourselves therefore under the mighty hand of God, that he may exalt you in due time' (I Peter 5.6). 'Humble yourselves in the sight of the Lord, and he shall exalt you' (James 4.10).

That the whole life of man is viewed from the point of view of obedience to God needs no further evidence.[2] It may suffice to refer to one statement: 'To the mind of late Judaism religion is *obedience*. Humble, servile submission of the human will to God's almighty, inscrutable will, acting according to his commandments, comprehensible or incomprehensible, at every moment of life— this is piety'.[3] That is why in contrast with Greek literature where the word is used only of the vile and despised behaviour of the real slave, in the OT the expression 'servant' or 'slave' becomes the decisive word to denote all service. It is the description which is typical of the behaviour of a religious man, and it has the title 'Lord' as its complement.[4] All the great patriarchs of the OT are called 'servants of God': Abraham, Isaac, Jacob (=Israel!),

[1] *Str-B.*, I, p. 249 f., 774. A whole series of further examples p. 192 ff., 921. Cf. also *Test. Abr.*, 7.10.

[2] Cf. W. D. Davies, *Paul and Rabbinic Judaism*, 1948, p. 259 ff. (on the atoning suffering of the righteous one, p. 262 ff.). R. Mach, *Der Zaddik in Talmud und Midrasch*, 1957, gives many examples of the idea of obedience and the idea of reward.

[3] W. Bousset—H. Gressmann, *Die Religion des Judentums* (*Handbuch*), Tübingen, 1926, p. 375.

[4] Δουλεύειν τῷ κυρίῳ is the characteristic expression for all that the righteous one does: Ps. 2.11; 99.2; 101.23. Cf. on the whole subject H. Rengstorf in *Th.Wb.* II, p. 268 ff.

Moses, Joshua, David, the prophets. The same usage is found in the NT, though here Jesus often takes God's place as the 'Lord'. Here too the faithful, especially the prophets in the Revelation, the saints in Acts and in I Peter, the aged Simeon in Luke's Infancy narrative are called the 'servants' of God, and the expression becomes even more frequent in the Apostolic Fathers.

But the title 'son' also is above all determined by the motive of obedience. Israel is called to be the 'firstborn son' of God, 'that he may serve me' (Ex. 4.22 f.). Mal. 1.6 regards the relationship of a son to his father as parallel to that of a slave to his lord: 'A son honoureth his father, and a servant his master: where then is mine honour?' and ch. 3.17 regards service as characteristic of sonship: 'I will spare them, as a man spareth his own son that serveth him.'[1]

Besides all this especial emphasis is placed on the value of *suffering*. Again just a few examples will suffice: 'He who offers his back to chastisement will become clean; for the Lord is kind to those that take chastisement upon themselves' (Psalms of Solomon 10.2). 'If thou desirest life, then look for chastisement.' Therefore Rabbi Akibah (*circa* A.D. 100) does not rejoice until his teacher suffers.[2] The righteous, above all others, are those whom Satan continually accuses, they alone are led into temptation. It therefore holds good: 'Everyone who rejoices in his suffering brings salvation to the world.' Actually the righteous ought not to die, but they voluntarily accept death and receive double reward in the hereafter.[3] The evidence for the high valuation of voluntary martyrdom and its reward has already been collected by others.[4]

Of particular importance is the *atoning power* of suffering, first of all for one's own sins: the righteous suffer on account of their sins, but the others will be punished by God's judgment (II Macc. 7.18 f., 32 ff.). Of the most severe sin, blasphemy, it is said:

[1] Cf. also O. Cullmann, *The Christology of the New Testament*, London, 1959, p. 272 ff.

[2] *Str-B.*, II, p. 278; I, p. 390.

[3] GenR. 84.100[3] and MG Gen.37.1, p. 622 (Mach, p. 95); GenR. 55.585 (Mach, p. 97); Joshua ben Levi, Taan.8a (Mach, p. 96); GenR. 9.71 (Mach, p. 150). Cf. *Syr. Bar.*, 52.6 f. and J. Sanders, *Suffering as divine discipline in the OT and post-biblical Judaism*, Colgate Rochester Divinity School Bulletin xxviii, 1955, special issue, p. 105 ff.

[4] *Str-B.*, I, p. 224 ff.

'Repentance and the day of atonement provide one-third part of atonement, suffering on the other days of the year another third, and the day of death provides complete atonement.'[1]- Someone who is being executed declares: 'If I am not guilty of this, then may my death atone for all my sins'.[2] Or God speaks: 'I will chastise thee with suffering in the present world in order to cleanse thee from sin for the world to come'.[3] The idea that the suffering and death of the righteous also atone vicariously for the sins of others is so widespread that we will only mention where to find the evidence.[4] The righteous of the Qumran sect also achieve atonement for the world through the tribulations of the time of purification.[5]

Similarly thoughts of the *exaltation* of the righteous one were a living issue. We have already quoted some examples. That a great reward is awaiting them is self-evident and needs no special proof. The following may be quoted as referring more particularly to the idea of exaltation: It is said of the righteous one that 'as soon as he has endured the temptation God raises him to the position of a ruler'.[6] Already during their life-time in the midst of their sufferings the righteous are higher in God's sight than the angels. Therefore they will be higher than the angels in the world to come[7] and a seat will be reserved for them in heaven.[8] In that world they will be the 'children of exaltation'[9] and will take part in the Last Judgment as judges[10] and executors of the Judgment.[11]

[1]Cf. also E. Lohse, *Märtyrer und Gottesknecht*, 1955, p. 29 ff.

[2]*Str-B.*, I, p. 636 f. (parallels 114, 142, 417 f.).

[3]R. Meir (*ca.* A.D. 150); also R. Eleazar ben Zadok (*ca.* 100) speaks similarly: *Str-B.*, II, p. 277 ff.; with special reference to the righteous one while the wicked suffer a converse fate, cf. R. Akiba (until *ca.* 135); *Str.-B.*, I, p. 390 (parallels here and in vol. II, p. 278).

[4]II Macc. 7.37 f.; IV Macc. 1.11; 6.28 f.; 17.20 ff.; *Str-B.*, II, pp. 278–82; I, p. 757; J. Jeremias in *Th.Wb.*, IV, p. 858 f.; G. F. Moore, *Judaism in the first Centuries of the Christian Era*, Cambridge, 1927, i, p. 546 ff.; E. Best, *One Body in Christ*, London, 1955, p. 206.

[5]*I QS* (Manual of Discipline), 5.6; 8.3 f., 10; 9.4; cf. I QSa, 1.3; I Q 22.iv.1 (?) = D. Barthélemy—J. T. Milik, Qumran Cave I, p. 95.

[6]Tanch. B. behaalotecha 13 (Mach, p. 97).

[7]*Str-B.*, III, p. 673; IV, p. 1140, 1153.

[8]Philo, *De execrat.* 6 (*Str-B.*, III, p. 291); IV Macc. 17.5.

[9]Sanh. 97b. 33 (R. Simeon ben Jochai, A.D. 150).

[10]Dan. 7.22, LXX; Wisdom 3.8, and rabbin. passages (*Str.-B.*, IV, p. 871 f.; 1103 f.; cf. II, p. 543; also Matt. 19.28; Luke 22.30; I Cor. 6.2).

[11]*Str-B.*, IV, p. 1095 (cf. 1107).

That is how the 'throne of glory' (I Sam. 2.8; Dan. 7.27) has been prepared for Israel. Therefore it is no cause for wonder that in the hour of death angels come to meet the righteous one[1] and that his countenance will be immediately transfigured.[2]

This exaltation can take place in the form of an *ascension*, or rather an assumption, a being carried away into heaven. This of course is found as early as II Kings 2 and probably also Gen. 5.24. In I Macc. 2.58 the assumption of Elijah is definitely regarded as a reward for his zeal for the Law. This thought can be found frequently in Jewish Apocrypha.[3] The idea of an ascension is first found in the form of a vision (Ethiopic Book of Enoch 39.3; 52.1; but cf. 81.5). The Greek Apocalypse of Baruch 2 ff. speaks of a journey through five heavens and a return to earth. Something similar is found in the Testament of Levi 2–5; the Slavonic Book of Enoch 3; 7 f.; 11; Testament of Abraham 7.19; 8.1 ff., etc. In the Tract Pesachim a vision in a feverish condition is described, 50a.[4] Later scepticism in respect of such experiences is expressed J. Taan. 2.1.[5] More relevant are the many passages describing a real assumption of the righteous one into heaven.[6] The righteous one as a whole man, body and soul, is 'carried away' (Jubilees 4.23), 'withdrawn from human sight' (IV Ezra 14.9, 49), 'lifted up' (Ethiopic Enoch 89.52; 90.31) and placed in a new position. In future he is allowed to live with God (Ethiopic Enoch 89.52) or his Messiah-Servant (IV Ezra 14.9). In virtue of his righteousness (Ethiopic Enoch 71.14; Jubilees 10.17) Enoch becomes the clerk of the heavenly court who keeps the

---

[1] *Str-B.*, IV, p. 894; II, p. 139.

[2] Many examples in *Str-B.*, I, p. 673 f.; 752; IV, p. 1138 f. In the Messianic era the righteous will give light: IV, p. 891. This is the divine splendour which once was found on the face of Adam and which will be renewed in the new world: IV, p. 887.

[3] For the Hellenistic parallels cf. the examples given in *Erniedrigung und Erhöhung*, ch. 15b; also *Reallexikon für Antike und Christentum* I, p. 30, L. Gernet in *Anthropologie Religieuse*, ed. C. J. Bleeker, 1955, p. 53 ff.

[4] *Str-B.*, III, p. 531. Cf. also Chagiga 14b ff.; Irenaeus, *adv. haer.* V.5.1.

[5] 'If a man says . . . I ascend to heaven, he will not do it' (quoted by E. Stauffer, *Theologie des neuen Testaments*, Gütersloh, 1945, note 440; Engl. ed. *New Testament Theology* trans. by J. Marsh, London, 1955, p. 289).

[6] Stauffer, p. 329 (Appendix vi) (Engl. ed., p. 344); H. Odeberg, *Th.Wb.* II, p. 554 f.; for Moses: E. Schürer, *Geschichte des jüdischen Volkes*, III⁴, Leipzig, p. 303; cf. H. Bickermann, 'Das leere Grab', *ZNW*, 23, 1924, p. 281 f.; H. Windisch, 'Der Hebräerbrief' (*Handbuch z. N.T.*), Tübingen, 1931², p. 70 f.

books (Jub. 4.23). Baruch is 'kept' as a witness to the Last Judgment (Syriac Apocalypse of Baruch 13.3); it is said of Adam (The Assumption of Moses 39; Vita Ad. (Life of Adam and Eve) 47) that he 'will be returned to his dominion' and 'will sit on the throne of him who has deceived him.' According to Slavonic Enoch 22.4–10 Enoch is appointed the archangel who stands by the side of God's throne (cf. 55.2, 67). It is understandable that eventually the Ascension of Isaiah 9.6 ff. as well as John 3.13 say in correction—there is only *one* exaltation, that of Christ.[1]

A particular problem is raised by chapters 70 ff. of Ethiopian Enoch in which the ascension of Enoch is related. 'The name of the Son of man was raised aloft to the Lord of spirits' (70.1),[2] ascends into heaven, yea into the heaven of heavens (71.1, 5). There his body is dissolved and his spirit is changed, until the Ancient of days addresses him as the 'Son of man' and promises him that the heritage of 'all who walk in his ways' will be with him in all eternity (71.11, 14, 16).[3] This view is incompatible with the other parabolic addresses where the elected Son of man is pre-existent in heaven. Later Christianity could of course combine both views and regard the Son of man as the image of Christ.[4]

Nowhere else is there any question of a humiliation and exaltation of the *Messiah* or the Son of man. The rabbinic exegesis of Ps. 110.1[5] mentions only his appointment as a Teacher of the Law, and the same text is perhaps referred to when

---

[1]According to Asc. Is. the ascended righteous will not receive their (garments), thrones and crowns until after the exaltation of Christ. This is probably an attack on such views as those in Hebr. Enoch, according to which the righteous one even becomes a 'little Yahveh' (Ed. H. Odeberg, Cambridge, 1928, pp. 82, 123, 141, 188 f.; cf. 35.6, p. 119). The idea of the assumption is spiritualized by Philo, *Quis rer. div. haer.* 276: The death of the wise man is merely a departure. Cf. also the ascension of the Lord (= God) in *The Rest of the Words of Baruch* (ed. Rendel Harris, London, 1889), 3.13.

[2]According to the oldest manuscripts (M. Black, *JThSt*, 1952, 4).

[3]According to Mowinckel this is no more than the assumption of the righteous Enoch who receives a heavenly reward for his righteousness; cf. E. Sjöberg, *Der Menschensohn im äthiopischen Henochbuch*, 1946, p. 150 ff. F. S. Mowinckel, *He that cometh*, Oxford, 1956, p. 437 ff.

[4]M. Black, *JTS*, n.s. III (1952), p. 1 ff. has recently described chs. 70 f. as the oldest part of the parabolic addresses. He believes that they represent the belief in the 'Head of the elect' describing the immortalized patriarch who is at the beginning and the end of history.

[5]*Str-B.*, IV, p. 918.

Enoch's Son of man is said to sit on God's throne and to hold judgment.[1]

The description of the humiliation and exaltation of the righteous one may be represented once more by a document of pre-Christian Hellenistic Judaism, the first chapters of the Wisdom of Solomon: How do the ungodly speak? 'Let us oppress the poor righteous man. The very sight of him is a nuisance to us. . . . He prides himself on having knowledge of God and calls himself God's servant. . . . He boasts that God is his Father. Let us see if his words are true and let us prove what shall happen in the end of him. For if the righteous one is a son of God, then God will have mercy upon him and deliver him from the hands of his adversaries. Let us try him with jeering and ill-treatment that we may get to know his meekness and test his steadfastness. Let us condemn him to a dishonourable death; for according to his words he will be protected' (2.10, 14, 13, 16–20). But the righteous look forward to the 'reward for blameless souls' (2.22). They are, it is true, 'punished in the sight of men', but 'having been a little chastised, they shall be greatly rewarded: for God proved them, and found them worthy for himself' (3.4 f.). Thus 'they shall shine, and run to and fro like sparks among the stubble. They shall judge the nations, and have dominion over the people, and their Lord shall reign for ever. . . . Grace and mercy is to his saints, and he hath care for his elect. But the ungodly shall be punished' (3.7–10). 'He pleased God, and was beloved of him: so that living among sinners he was translated' (4.10). 'The people saw, and understood it not, neither laid they up this in their minds, That his grace and mercy is with his saints, and that he hath respect unto his chosen. Thus the righteous that is dead shall condemn the ungodly which are living. . . . They shall see the end of the wise, and shall not understand what God in his counsel hath decreed of him, and to what end the Lord hath set him in safety . . .' (4.15 ff.). But in the last days shall 'the righteous man stand in great boldness before the face of such as have afflicted him, and made no account of his labours. When they see it, they shall be troubled with terrible fear, and shall be

[1]Chs. 45.3; 49.4; 51.3; 55.4; 61.8; 62.2–5; 69.27, 29. When R. Akiba (d. about 135) spoke of David's sitting on the divine throne this was regarded as a profanation of the deity (*Str.-B.*, I, p. 978). But cf. p. 31, n. 1.

amazed at the strangeness of his salvation. . . . How is he numbered among the children of God, and his lot is among the saints.' (5.1–5). 'But the righteous live for evermore; their reward also is with the Lord, and the care of them is with the most High. Therefore shall they receive a glorious kingdom. . . .' (5.15 f.).[1]

The way of the righteous one depicted here is even in many details the way which Jesus has actually gone.[2]

We can now summarize: Judaism frequently speaks of the righteous one who humbles himself or who voluntarily accepts humiliation by suffering and death in obedience to God. Suffering in particular is very valuable as atonement for one's own sins or vicarious atonement for other people's. As a reward the righteous one is exalted by God, secretly already on earth, but especially in the world to come, where he finds his seat reserved for him in heaven, the throne of glory, and there acts as a judge and executioner. This exaltation can also be pictured physically as an assumption from the earth, as an ascension to heaven.

It is different with the Messiah who is not to be exalted but whose Lordship is merely to be revealed at the end of time. He either rules as an earthly King over the Servant Israel (Ps. Sol.), or he appears as the Judge and Saviour in heaven. As such he already lives with God beforehand (Ethiopian Enoch; IV Ezra). He destroys all the enemies which attack him and all the evil spirits (Ethiopian Enoch; IV Ezra), takes his place on the throne of glory (Ethiopian Enoch; Syriac Baruch), forms the new Congregation of the elect, reigns over them and lives with them on a new earth under a new heaven (Ethiopian Enoch; IV Ezra in part). According to Rabbinic tradition he is placed at God's right hand to be a Teacher of the Law.

[1]For the connexion with Deut.–Isa., cf. M. J. Suggs, 'Wisdom of Solomon, 2.10–15, a homily based on the fourth Servant Song' (*JBL*, 76, 1957, pp. 26–33).

[2]Cf. Wisdom 2.13, 18–20 with Matt. 27.43 (also Wisdom 4.19 with Acts 1.18). A similar description of the suffering and redemption of the righteous one is found in I QH 2.8 ff., 32 ff. M. Philonenko (*Theol. Zeitschrift*, Basle, 1958, p. 81 ff.) thinks, therefore, that Wisdom 2.10 ff. describes the teacher of righteousness of Qumran. This would be interesting, because it would show that the righteous of Wisdom 2–5 was originally meant as a definite individual, not as the type of all the righteous ones. But this remains very uncertain. Cf. *Revue d'Histoire et de Philos. rel.* 1958, p. 309 ff.

On the other hand the term Son of man includes humility[1] as well as an eschatological *rôle*. In Ethiopian Enoch, at any rate, his exaltation to heaven, where all his followers will share his heritage, is awaited.

[1]Cf. especially for the term in Ezekiel, W. Eichrodt in *EvTh*, 1959, p. 1 ff. That Ezekiel had been of prime importance is mentioned particularly by E. M. Sidebottom, 'The Son of man in the Fourth Gospel', *Exp. Times*, 68 pp. 231 ff., 280 ff. For Daniel cf. C. K. Barrett in *N.T. Essays*, ed. A. J. B. Higgins, Manchester, 1959, p. 1 ff.; for a survey of the whole problem Higgins, *ibid.*, p. 119 ff.; Mowinckel, *He that cometh*, p. 346 ff.

III

JESUS AS THE SUFFERING AND EXALTED RIGHTEOUS ONE

DID the early Church regard Jesus in the light of this picture, familiar to her, of the Righteous One whom God leads into suffering and humiliation, but whom he exalts after his death?

Jesus himself promised the disciples whom he called to follow him, that they would go with him in the way of humility and humiliation, that perhaps, with him, they might lose their lives in order to receive them again from God, and now for the first time in a true sense. He himself and his disciples with him have expected that in the coming Kingdom he would be exalted by God to particular honour and that this exaltation would also be extended to those who followed him (Luke 22.28–30). Through the death of Jesus and above all through his appearances to the disciples this could only become more clearly outlined. Is it possible to find traces of such belief in the tradition of the early Church?

We have no direct transmission from this time. Peter's sermons in Acts are essentially creations of the author.[1] But it cannot be disputed that he has used ancient material, especially in the short christological summaries, even though we are no longer able to verify to what extent. And here we find the Jewish title 'the Righteous One' which is frequent in Rabbinic as well as in apocalyptic literature.[2] In Acts 3.14 Jesus is called 'the Holy and

[1] Cf. Ed. Schweizer, *Theol. Zeitschrift*, Basle, 1957, p. 1 ff. Reasons for this appreciation of the tradition are given in *Erniedrigung und Erhöhung*, p. 45, note 180.

[2] G. Schrenk, *Th.Wb.* II, p. 188 f. For the title 'Righteous One' cf. H. J. Schoeps, *Theologie und Geschichte des Judenchristentums*, Tübingen, 1949, p. 143; A. Descamps, *Les justes et la justice dans les évangiles et le christianisme primitif*, Louvain, 1950, p. 69 ff.; interpreted as a royal title by H. Riesenfeld, *Jésus transfiguré*, Copenhagen, 1947, p. 77. According to Descamps, p. 59 ff., Acts 3.14 originally describes Jesus simply as innocent in the sense of the Jewish righteous one; the author of the Acts was the first to interpret δίκαιος as a Messianic title.

Righteous One', and the title 'the Righteous One' also occurs chs. 7.52; 22.14, in both cases in traditional material. In all three passages it is at least *also* assumed that he has shown himself to be righteous especially by his innocent death.[1] At all events it can be stated with certainty that in Peter's sermons the death on the cross has no atoning significance. It is the inevitable condition, suffered in obedience, of the exaltation to glory. The stereotyped expression 'You have slain him,[2] God has raised him' underlines this very thought that it is as the One who is rejected by men and cast down into humiliation and shame that Jesus has been exalted by God. Even where the earthly Jesus is referred to as a miracle-worker (Acts 2.22; 10.38) he is merely an instrument in God's service (as are the Apostles, Acts 15.4, 12).

The title 'the Righteous One' is also to be found elsewhere. In a characteristically traditional expression, I Peter 3.18, it is said of Christ that he suffered for sins *once*, 'the righteous for the unrighteous'. Here the idea of vicarious suffering has already been adopted. But here too his righteousness is shown by his suffering, and, what is more, by his innocent suffering. I Peter 1.10 speaks of his passion and the glory that follows. As a 'Righteous One' Jesus is, according to I John 2.1, the 'Advocate with the Father' and according to I John 2.29; 3.7 is accompanied by a Church which follows him in righteousness.[3] And according to John 5.30 Jesus' judgment is righteous because he does nothing by himself but in all things is obedient to the Father.[4]

More relevant is another observation. Though the title 'Righteous One' is virtually absent from the Synoptic tradition[5] there is no doubt that the early Church has seen Jesus in the character of the Righteous One suffering in obedience. The Passion story was the first to be written down. The liturgical

---

[1]Cf. the textually disputed expression αἷμα δίκαιον Matt. 27.4 and G. Schrenk in *Th.Wb.* II, p. 190 f.

[2]Cf. the formulation in James 5.6 which originates from the group of Jewish statements on the suffering righteous one: 'Ye have condemned, ye have killed the righteous one; he doth not resist you.'

[3]Here, however, the word is no longer used absolutely, as a title, but as an attribute.

[4]Paul may have avoided this title because it comes in too close proximity to righteousness through the Law (W. L. Knox, *The Acts of the Apostles,* Cambridge, 1948, p. 73).

[5]It is only to be found in Matt. 27.19 (24?); Luke 23.47.

formula adopted by Paul, I Cor. 11.23, already presupposes a knowledge of the events of the Passion when it begins: 'The same night in which he was betrayed. . . .' This shows that at a very early date the account of this event was considered essential by the Church. This is amazing because at the same time it must be said that an explanation of the Passion, in the sense of propitiation or vicarious suffering, is hardly to be found within the Synoptic tradition.[1] It seems almost as if it was regarded as a matter of course that Jesus was led in this way. Only the divine 'must' is expressly underlined, particularly in the most primitive and probably earliest formulations.[2] The decisive element in the suffering is seen in the scorn to which Jesus was exposed.[3] That is the humiliation which the Righteous One in Israel suffers.[4]

Even more decisive is a second observation. The earliest account of the Passion is interspersed with reminiscences of the Old Testament, especially derived from the Psalms of suffering. This is not due to apologetic attempts of the early Church to justify God's way to her enemies or even to her own doubts, for in the Gospel according to Mark there is as yet no indication that all this has been prophesied in the OT. OT sentences or phrases come in here as yet without comment. This shows that to the early Church the first book of the Passion of Jesus was formed by the Psalms of the suffering of the Righteous One.[5] This is even true of the Gospel according to John where the Psalms of the deliverance of the suffering Righteous One (Ps. 22.19, 16(?); 69.22; 34.21) serve to illustrate this Passion.[6] As with the Righteous One in Israel, here also the suffering is the unavoidable gateway to glory: the story of the Passion is followed by the story of Easter.[7]

[1]Mark 10.45; 14.24 will be discussed later (p. 50).
[2]Cf. also Luke 22.37; 24.26, 44; Matt. 26.54.
[3]Mark 9.12; 15.16 ff., 29 ff.; Luke 23.11 f.; cf. Heb. 12.2; 13.13.
[4]Ps. 22.8; Isa. 50. 6 f.; 53.3 and frequently.
[5]Lohmeyer, *Markus*, p. 343.
[6]I agree with C. H. Dodd, *The Interpretation of the Fourth Gospel*, Cambridge, 1953, p. 233 f. that John 19.36 can be regarded as dependent on Ps. 34.21. But I disagree with him in thinking that this holds good only of the tradition used by the evangelist, while the latter himself thought of Ex. 12.46; Num. 9.12; cf. ch. 1.29 and on this passage C. K. Barrett, 'The Lamb of God' (*N.T. Studies*, I, 1954–5, p. 210 ff.).
[7]Cf. also the idea of a baptism in death as a gateway to glory, Mark 10.38; Luke 12.50.

More difficult to appreciate is the story of the Temptation. It follows the story of the Baptism[1] in the same way as the temptation of Adam follows his appointment as a ruler in God's service. Above all however in the short version of Mark Jesus is depicted as the second Adam. As, according to the Midrash, Adam is venerated by wild beasts[2] and fed by angels,[3] so also is Jesus. In him the state of paradise has been restored.[4] Ps. 91.11–13 already says of the righteous one that the wild beasts surround him and the angels serve him. Above all, however, reference should be made to the Testament of Naphtali 8 where the righteous one is promised that the devils will flee from him, the wild beasts will fear him and the angels will take care of him. Jesus is depicted as the perfect Righteous One who resists the temptation and who thereby as a second Adam brings about the state of paradise. He is the 'eschatological Righteous One'.[5]

Beside this we would refer to the scene in Gethsemane which describes the obedience of Jesus, prepared to suffer. Finally we find among the most frequently used and most varied words of Jesus those which refer to his service: 'I am in the midst of you as he that serveth' (Luke 22.27). 'The Son of man came

---

[1]Here the aspect of humiliation would be strongly emphasized if the original form of God's words had been: 'Thou art my servant' (J. Jeremias, *Th.Wb.* V, p. 699). But even if, still in imitation of Ps. 2.7, the words described the appointment of the Son of God, that is to say the King (which seems more probable to me), the emphasis is still on the call of *service* to God (cf. p. 25). This may be the reason why Isa. 42.1 is added here.

[2]*Apoc. Mos.* 16; J. Jeremias, *Th.Wb.*, I, p. 141. According to *Apoc. Mos.* 10 f. the dominion of the wild beasts began after the fall of Eve; according to Isa. 11.6 f. and Rabbinic sources (*Str-B.*, IV, p. 527) the Messiah is to make an end of it.

[3]*Vit. Ad.* 4; *Bab. Sanh.* 59b and par. (cited by J. Jeremias, *Th.Wb.*, I, p. 141). Other interesting features are found in *Vit. Ad.*: Adam fasts for forty days standing in the river Jordan as penitence for his fall (ch. 6; 17); he is surrounded by all (aquatic) animals (8). The devil, changed into a shining figure, tempts Eve (9) and complains to Adam that he fell from heaven because he did not want to worship him, Adam (12 f.).

[4]Gen. 1.26; Isa. 11.6–8; 65.25.

[5]The importance of the narrative of the temptation for the whole of Mark's Gospel is emphasized by J. M. Robinson, *Das Geschichtsverständnis des Markusevangeliums*, 1956, pp. 25–33; *The Problem of History in Mark*, London, 1957, pp. 28–32. J. Dupont's view that Jesus is regarded as a second Moses (*N.T. Studies*, III, 1957, p. 287 ff.) may be right as far as Matt. and Luke are concerned, but scarcely holds good for the short account of Mark which I consider more original and which I think is to be understood as above.

not to be ministered unto but to minister' (Mark 10.45).[1]

Already in the Synoptic Gospels much must remain unclear until one recognizes how naturally Jesus' life was at first regarded as the fate of the Righteous One in Israel. Only so do we understand that the inevitableness of suffering is simply stated without any attempt at explanation and that the exaltation follows equally as a matter of course; that the story of the temptation before Q contains no trace of specifically Messianic temptations[2] but simply relates the temptations of the righteous one; that references to passages about the Servant of God, it is true, are relatively frequent but that in the tradition the atoning suffering of Isa. 53 did not spread widely as a central concept to explain the Passion of Jesus.[3]

Before we trace the effects of this view of the passion of Jesus in the NT we have to ask whether in the early Church Easter was also interpreted in the sense of the exaltation of the Righteous One.

If Jesus did foresee suffering and rejection for himself and his disciples, then, of course, he saw it not as a catastrophe but as a gateway to the glory of the coming Kingdom. If he did call himself the Son of man and connected this title with his lowly state on earth as well as with the glory to come,[4] then he must in fact have expected something like his exaltation to the presence of God.[5] That the Easter events have been understood by the early Church to this effect can still be verified. Acts 2.36 establishes that this exaltation to God first 'made Jesus Lord and Christ'. This is certainly not Lucan theology but as yet a very primitive view which, in Rome. 1.3, Paul has already corrected. The combination of the two titles may have come from Ps. 2.2. The same Psalm is referred to also in Acts 13.33, again in a sermon of similar style. Here the resurrection of Jesus is regarded as his appointment to sonship of God, by which the promise is fulfilled: 'Thou art my

---

[1]Cf. the various forms of the saying 'If any man would be first, he shall be last of all, and minister of all' (Mark 9.35; cf. 10.43 f. par.; Matt. 23.11).

[2]Bultmann, *Syn. Tradition*, p. 272 ff.

[3]Cf. p. 49 ff.

[4]Cf. p. 39 ff.

[5]This would be even more obvious if J. A. T. Robinson (*Jesus and His Coming*, pp. 43–47) is right in saying that Jesus expected his vindication in the sense of Dan. 7.13 f. Cf. p. 40, n. 2.

Son, this day I have begotten thee.' Finally the same notion occurs in Rom. 1.4 in a formula which is certainly old and which Paul must have received through the tradition,[1] where Jesus' resurrection originally was regarded as his appointment as the Son of God. How old this notion is can be gathered from two facts. For one thing Paul already corrects this quotation by making 'the Son of God' the superscription of the whole formula, that is to say by claiming this title even for the earthly Jesus. Moreover this formula which is quoted by Paul at the very beginning of his epistle because it was evidently widely known at the time he wrote, already has a good deal of early Christian doctrinal history behind it. The view that only the exaltation of Jesus to God made him the Son of God[2] has here already been harmonized with another tradition which saw Jesus' life upon earth in the light of the traditional Jewish expectation of the Messiah. The harmonization has been effected by regarding the earthly Jesus as the Davidic Messiah-King (more or less in the sense of the Ps. Sol.) and the exalted Jesus as the actual Son of God. All this, of course, has nothing to do with later Adoptianism. For the Church had not yet *reflected* on the time before the exaltation and therefore did not say that Jesus had been merely an ordinary man. These formulations prove only that at a very early time the exaltation of Jesus was regarded as the decisive saving event. In this first period this was so important to the Church that all that preceded it was regarded as a mere prelude to this one event.

This precisely is the view which the sermons of Peter still convey to us.

What happened at Easter overwhelmed the Church to such an extent that it dominated all its thought and became the very centre of all its preaching. The resurrection of Jesus confirmed that they had been right when they followed him. They were right and not their opponents. His life was the life of the Righteous, the Obedient One whose part God had now taken. His death therefore was no failure but the fulfilment of God's will.

[1] That Jesus is the Son of David, a thought which is not found elsewhere in Paul's writings, is the main point here, while the cross is not mentioned. Non-Pauline expressions are ὁρίζειν (Acts 10.42; 17.31!) and πνεῦμα ἁγιοσύνης (Ps. 51.13; Isa. 63.10 f.; *Test. Levi* 18.11).

[2] Cf. also Hermas, *Sim.* V, 2.7, 11 and 6.5–7, and on this M. Dibelius, *Der Hirt des Hermas*, Tübingen, 1923, pp. 564 f., 573 f.

And his resurrection was the divine exaltation of the Righteous One. The idea of 'exaltation' in Acts 2.33, 36; 5.31 interprets that of 'resurrection'. It means the appointment of Jesus as 'Lord and Christ', as 'Son', the enthronement 'on God's right hand' (Acts 2.33 ff.; 5.31). Also, according to Acts 7.55 f., the Exalted One appears on God's right hand. Always the exaltation is mentioned in immediate connexion with his death in humiliation; it is God's reply to the latter.

That the exaltation of Jesus really dominated the thought of the early Church is also shown by the fact that the oldest tradition barely distinguishes between Easter and Ascension. It is even doubtful if the mention of the forty days (Acts 1.3) is not a later gloss. In any case according to Luke 24.51 the ascension takes place on Easter Day.[1] But however this may be, at all events in the Gospel according to St Matthew the risen Christ appears to his disciples as the One to whom all authority in heaven and on earth has already been given (Matt. 28.18). Also according to John (John 20.17) the ascension takes place on Easter morning before the appearances. It may well be asked if the reports of the first appearances (I Cor. 15.5 f.) have been lost because they told of Jesus' exaltation to God and on account of that were not sufficiently realistic in the eyes of a later generation. At any rate this would explain that Paul places his appearance on the road to Damascus entirely on the same level as the appearances to the twelve.[2]

The word 'exaltation' is not found in the Synoptic Gospels. This is what might be expected as altogether they contain few Christological statements. In particular the resurrection or exaltation of Jesus is barely considered. Where it is mentioned it receives no further interpretation. We would here simply refer to the passages already mentioned, where Jesus' death in rejection and shame

[1]This is independent of whether one regards the words '. . . and was carried up into heaven' as authentic or not; for Acts 1.2 at any event presupposes this interpretation. The same holds good of (Mark) 16.19. Barnabas 15.9 still places the ascension on Easter Sunday and so do a great number of early Christian passages (cf. H. Windisch, *Der Barnabasbrief*, Tübingen, 1920, p. 385).
[2]Luke with his interpretation of the appearances of course had to deny this; but even he does not emphasize the difference but stresses the fact that the original apostles are those who have accompanied Jesus upon earth (Acts 1.22).

and his resurrection follow one another as a matter of course, just as it also holds good of the disciples that he who gives up his life is precisely the one who will find it.

But the view that the event of Easter was the appointment to heavenly glory can still be traced behind the Synoptic tradition of the resurrection.[1] This is the case especially with the Son of man tradition.[2] A careful and thorough going analysis of all the Synoptic passages leads to the following astonishing facts[3]: 1. The *parousia* passages do not seem to be genuine, but much is to be said in favour of the view that behind our texts a stage can be detected in which the coming of the Son of man with the clouds of heaven was related to the exaltation and vindication of Jesus.[4] 2. The eschatological role of the Son of man seems to be originally that of the decisive witness accusing or saving men in the Last Judgment. 3. The sayings which describe Jesus as walking on earth in humility[5] rejected by an unbelieving people can be traced back to Jesus himself with the greatest degree of certainty.

In the Fourth Gospel we find a special layer which speaks about the Son of man and can be detached easily from the other

[1]Cf. G. Bertram, *Die Himmelfahrt Jesu vom Kreuz aus und der Glaube an seine Auferstehung, Festgabe für Ad. Deissmann*, 1927, pp. 187–217.

[2]Cf. p. 18; p. 22, n.2; p. 31, n. 1; p. 44. Recent literature in W. Bauer, *Wörterbuch zum neuen Testament*, Berlin, 1952, p. 1516 f. and in C. C. MacCown, 'Jesus, Son of man,' *Journal of Religion*, 1948, p. 1 ff.; also T. Arvedson, *Das Mysterium Christi*, Uppsala, 1938, p. 116 ff.; C. K. Barrett, S.J.T. vi. 1953, p. 232 ff.; M. Black, *Exp. Times* lx, 1948–9, p. 32 ff.; Dodd, *Fourth Gospel*, p. 241 ff., 411; Fuller, *Mission*, p. 95 ff.; A. Feuillet, 'Le fils de l'homme de Daniel et la tradition biblique,' R. *Biblique*, 1953, p. 170 ff.; W. Manson. *Jesus the Messiah*, London, app. D; Percy, *Botschaft*, p. 225 ff.; Th. Preiss, *Le fils de l'homme*, 1951; Riesenfeld, *Jésus transfiguré*, p. 307 ff.; J. A. T. Robinson, *Jesus and His Coming*; W. Staerk, *Die Erlösererwartung in den östlichen Religionen, Soter* II, Stuttgart, 1938, p. 421 ff.; Taylor, *Names*, p. 25 ff.

[3]E. Schweizer, 'Der Menschensohn (Zur eschatologischen Erwartung Jesu),' *ZNW*, 1959, p. 185 ff.

[4]Cf. especially Mark 14.62. In so far I agree with J. A. T. Robinson (p. 22, n. 2), but I think that it is impossible to explain the actual form of the saying in this way. Mark of course interpreted it in the sense of the *parousia*. He may therefore have inverted the original sequence of the two statements. Cf. also Luke 22.69: 'But from *henceforth* shall the Son of man be seated at the right hand of the power of God.' Ch. 9.51 Jesus' 'being received up' includes both his death and his exaltation (cf. Acts 1.22) Luke 24.26 speaks of his 'suffering and entering into his glory'.

[5]Cf. p. 31, note 1.

tradition.[1] It goes back at least to a time before the development of the specific Johannine theology or to a group to which this has remained strange. These words are almost without exception characterized by the expectation of the exaltation and glorification of the Son of man and his role in the Last Judgment.

That Jesus called himself the Son of man remains extremely probable,[2] because there would not be any other explanation of the astonishing fact that this term appears about eighty times which are, with the exception of Act. 7.56 and the figurative use in Rev. 1.13 ff., severely restricted to sayings of Jesus himself.

---

[1]S. Schulz, *Untersuchungen zur Menschensohnchristologie im Johannesevangelium*, Göttingen 1957, p. 96 ff.

[2]R. Bultmann (*Theology of the New Testament*, Vol. 1, London, 1952, ch. 4.3) thinks that Jesus regarded himself as the last prophet announcing the coming Son of man, not himself as the coming one. His most important argument is the fact that the title seems to be more firmly connected with the statements on the heavenly glory and the *parousia* than with those regarding the earthly life of Jesus (also T. W. Manson, *The Teaching of Jesus*, Cambridge, 1931, p. 225 f.), but that announcements of the passion and resurrection are never linked with these statements of the glory or the *parousia*, indeed that 'I' and 'Son of man' sometimes appear to be separate (Mark 8.38 e.g.). But this argument falls down as soon as one recognizes that the *parousia* sayings are in fact not the original ones and that the form of Mark 8.38 and 14.62 has its origin in the conscious restraint with which Jesus spoke of himself as the 'Son of man', because only the follower can know what this means. Moreover the title 'Son of man' is not connected with the preaching of the coming Kingdom of God, because his eschatological role is that of a witness in the last judgment, not of the bringer of this Kingdom (cf. p. 22, n. 2). All that however which A. Schweitzer, *The Quest of the historical Jesus*, London, 1952, p. 338 ff. (cf. the enlarged 2nd German Edition, *Geschichte der Leben-Jesu Forschung*, Tübingen, 1913, p. 378 ff.) cites against Wrede speaks in favour of the view that Jesus regarded himself as the Son of man. Reference should also be made to Jesus' self-consciousness which far surpasses that of a prophet (he calls men to follow him; he places his 'I say unto you' beside the prophetic 'thus saith Yahveh'; he declares that he is more than the prophetic 'thus saith Yahveh'; he declares that he is more than Jonah and Solomon!). How could the death of a prophet have had such a shattering effect on the disciples? All they would have had to do was to wait for the coming Son of man and to proclaim even more energetically that Jesus had been *only* a prophet who had been executed just like John the Baptist. Then the experiences of the resurrection would have merely confirmed the certitude that even death could not separate the elect from the coming Kingdom (of John the Baptist it was also believed that he had risen!). To refer to oneself in the third person, especially by the expression 'that man', was usual at the time (II Cor. 12.2, and Manson, *Teaching*, p. 217 f.), although the use of the term 'Son of man' was an original formulation of Jesus (cf. E. Sjöberg in *Acta Orientalia* 21, 1950, p. 57 ff., 91 ff.; Mowinckel, *He that cometh*, p. 347, n.1.)

Conversely the title 'Christ' appears only four times (including John 17.3) in words of Jesus relating to himself none of which seem to be original, but which are very frequently on the lips of the Church. That the earliest community in Jerusalem regarded Jesus as the exalted Son of man is proved by Act. 7.56.[1] Thus the consequence is almost inevitable: Jesus spoke of himself as of the Son of man humiliated on earth, rejected by men, exalted by God out of all suffering and witnessing for or against those who will appear before the Throne of God in the Last Judgment.

The picture of the suffering and exalted Righteous One has therefore to a very great extent determined the Church's early understanding of Christ. It is certain that Jesus did not regard himself—nor did the disciples regard their Master—as merely *one* of the many suffering righteous ones. For none of those suffering righteous ones had ever called disciples to follow him. None had supposed that it would be more tolerable for Sodom and Gomorrah than for him who did not obey his call. None had declared that the disciple in his discipleship would have to give up father and mother, wife and child, hand and foot, indeed his own life in order to find life. None had used the term 'Son of man' as the title appropriate to his own state. At all times Jesus was to them *the* Righteous One. Before therefore we trace the further development of these views we have to ask: What does this mean? In what way did the Church understand the uniqueness of Jesus?

[1]The saying seems to be original. Not only is the term nowhere else used outside the words of Jesus, the conception of Jesus (or the Son of man) *standing* on the right hand of God is also without parallels.

IV

JESUS AS THE REPRESENTATIVE OF THE TRUE ISRAEL

JESUS himself and his disciples expected the end of this world and the beginning of the Kingdom of God. What happened to Jesus was unique because in him came the end of all the existing history of God's dealings with men and the transition to the Kingdom of God. Thereby Jesus' career was placed in an entirely new light. In Jesus the history of Israel, the way of the righteous one in the people of God, was repeated. As Israel is above all a *suffering* nation that is led through suffering to glory, so is Jesus. The Pharisees already wanted to represent the true Israel by rendering the obedience which all should render. But more is happening here. The self-assurance with which Jesus himself already speaks and acts shows that he understood his way as the final eschatological fulfilment of all that preceded. And the Church came to the same conclusion. After the Easter appearances at the latest she must have realized that this was the eschatological fulfilment of all suffering, that Jesus was *the* suffering Righteous One.[1]

From this two deductions can be drawn. The first is the obser-

---

[1] I still doubt very much whether an Oriental religious system of a suffering and rising king was widespread in Israel and exercised a great influence on it during a large part of its history. But this need not be discussed here. For at all events the figure of the suffering righteous one would be only a remote offshoot. And this alone had effect on the Church. Jesus was regarded as the Righteous One of the last days, the culminating Righteous One who fulfilled the way of Israel. In the oldest tradition he is definitely *not* a King, let alone King and Priest in one. The title 'High Priest' does not occur until the Epistle to the Hebrews, where it is taken from Ps. 110 (but cf. G. Friedrich, 'Beobachtungen zur messianischen Hohepriestererwartung in den Synoptikern', *ZThK*, 53, 1956, pp. 265 ff.). Accordingly ceremonial terminology is almost entirely absent from the oldest tradition, whereas conversely the strong emphasis on eschatology in the religious system referred to is not original.

vation, already emphasized by C. H. Dodd,[1] that already at a very early stage the Church as a matter of course applied to Jesus passages from the OT which referred to Israel. She did this long before she reached the stage of scribal reflection where she engaged in methodical exegesis. For this kind of application occurs relatively widely and is usually quite spontaneous.

In the same way the Church soon begins to use titles of honour belonging to Israel in connection with Jesus. This holds good particularly of the title 'Son of God'.[2] As Israel is God's son, so is Jesus. In later times this title has certainly been understood in a physical sense. But Acts 13.33 and Rom. 1.4, as well as Mark 1.11, show that the Church originally spoke of the *appointment* of Jesus as the Son of God. Moreover Acts 13.33 and Rom. 1.4 are closely connected with the concept of the exaltation of the Righteous One. The title therefore primarily referred to the exalted Lord who was appointed King, and was afterwards extended to the appointment at the time of the baptism in Jordan and to the earthly Jesus. This explains the part that Ps. 2 has played in all this. It was easy to transfer the title to the earthly Jesus. For in the first place Jesus himself knew about the unique character of his relationship to the Father.[3] But moreover to the Jews the title 'son' implies above all serving obedience.[4] Even though Ps. 2.7 refers to the appointment of a King, the King of Israel is in a position of obedience to Jahveh. That is why his appointment as King can mark the beginning of Jesus' service upon earth (Mark 1.11). For the Church has always felt his baptism to have been an act of self-humiliation on Jesus' part and has therefore more and more eliminated the impression of lowliness in the tradition. Consequently this baptism emphasizes Jesus'

[1] C. H. Dodd, *According to the Scriptures*, London, 1952, pp. 103, 113, 117–19.
[2] Cf. J. Bieneck, *Sohn Gottes als Christusbezeichnung der Synoptiker*, 1951; V. Taylor, *The Names of Jesus*, London, 1953, p. 52 ff.; R. H. Fuller, *The Mission and Achievement of Jesus*, London, 1954, p. 80 ff.; O. Cullmann, *Christology of the New Testament*, p. 272 ff.
[3] G. Schrenk in *Th.Wb.* V, p. 984 ff., and particularly J. Jeremias in *ThLZ*, 1954, p. 213 f.; and in *Synoptische Studien* (für A. Wikenhauser), München, 1953, p. 86 ff.
[4] Cf. p. 25, 37. In Judaism 'Son of God' is not a Messianic title (W. G. Kümmel, *Mélanges M. Goguel*, 1950, p. 130; Eth. Enoch 105.2 is lacking in the Greek text; for IV Ezra cf. *Th.Wb.* V, p. 680, note 196; *Str-B.* III, p. 19 contains no passage which is certainly old. Cullmann, *Christology*, p. 280 f. is not so decisive on this point).

readiness to take the step into humiliation[1] and to take on himself what God had commanded him.[2]

The title 'Son of man', with which we have already dealt, is a name given to the nation of Israel in Dan. 7.13, 27; and Ps. 80.16.[3] This already favours the suggestion that Jesus has in fact so called himself.[4] However it is true, that Jesus would hardly have used it in a collective sense,[5] but rather as a title which can describe on the one hand the impotence of man in general and on the other hand the dignity of the exalted One at the right hand of God. We certainly do not find any indication that Jesus himself already regarded himself as the One who steps into the place of the whole of Israel, in the sense that he is not merely an individual but includes the fellowship of his disciples within himself. In most places the word is plainly used in an individual sense. There is no place where a collective interpretation is necessary. And that in the days of Jesus the expression was already used to indicate the individual figure of the apocalyptic Saviour seems to me to be proved not only by Enoch[6] and IV Ezra 13.3 but also by the

[1]H. Braun, 'Entscheidende Motive in den Berichten über die Taufe Jesu von Markus bis Justin', *ZThK*, 50, 1953, p. 39 f.

[2]This is true for the Church's interpretation. What Jesus himself felt at his baptism we simply cannot know. Here I should be more cautious than Cullmann, *Christology*, pp. 66 ff., 283.

[3]Here parallel to the expression 'man of thy right hand'. This shows that the concept in itself is not collective but that an individual concept is applied to the nation. Cf. E. Stauffer, *Novum Testamentum* I, 1956, p. 81 ff.

[4]Cf. p. 39 ff.

[5]A survey by MacCown in the *Journal of Religion*, 1948, p. 8 ff. The collective interpretation is defended e.g. by H. Odeberg, *The Fourth Gospel*, Uppsala, 1929, p. 39 f. and elsewhere; Manson, *Teaching*, p. 227 ff.; in the *Journal of Ecclesiastical History* I, p. 5 ff. he surmises that the disciples had applied the predictions of the passion and resurrection to their community and that this was the reason why they were so surprised at the death of Jesus; in *Bull. J.Ryl.L.*, xxxii, 1950, p. 171 ff. he speaks of an oscillation between an individual and a corporate sense; to the same effect N. A. Dahl, *Das Volk Gottes*, Oslo, 1951, p. 90. The opposite view is defended by C. K. Barrett, *The Holy Spirit and the Gospel Tradition*, London, 1947, p. 154; Kümmel, *Verheissung und Erfüllung*, note 27; p. 39 f. (Engl. ed. pp. 27 and 46). Also E. Sjöberg, *Der verborgene Menschensohn in den Evangelien*, 1955, p. 241, note 1.

[6]It is true that all that we have here is the translation of a translation, in which we find three different renderings of 'the Son of man', so that we are on very uncertain ground. Yet it must be said that a Christian interpolator would scarcely have inserted varying expressions but rather one and the same: the one he found in the Bible. And is it really at all probable that at such a late date anyone would have interpolated a title which had long

Messianic interpretation of Dan. 7.13 in the LXX, in Rabbinic literature and in Rev. 1.13 f.[1] The element of truth in the mentioning of the collective meaning of the word however is this: that with this expression the thought of the congregation (or also the angels) around the exalted righteous One or Saviour quite easily plays some part. That holds good of Enoch (38.1 f.; 39.4–8; 71.16; perhaps 49.3) and IV Ezra (13.52) as well as of the NT. In the early Church this may have encouraged the view that in Jesus the whole history of Israel had come to its end.

We have therefore found the starting-point of a concept that has become extremely fruitful for the NT. Until now we have the representation of Israel by Jesus interpreted to the effect that he was, so to speak, the *end* of Israel's way, the One in whom was fulfilled what had previously appeared only in a fragmentary way.[2] But now new concepts of representation attach themselves to this. Jesus is the One who has gone to the end of Israel's way, through suffering to exaltation by God. This thought is adopted in John 15.1 ff., when Jesus is called 'the true Vine'. In the OT Israel is the vine of Jahveh, his 'son of man' (Ps. 80.16).[3] But at the same time Jesus is the One who has taken his disciples with him on this his way. This is taken up in John 15.1 ff. when this Vine at the same time includes in itself all its branches. New developments of thought certainly play their part here as well. First of all reference should be made to the old concept of the father of the tribe, according to which the progenitor already determines and anticipates the career of all the coming generations. This however had already changed under the influence of Hellenistic thought.[4] The

become obsolete within the Church instead of one which was still in use? In the Enoch fragments from Qumran nothing has so far been found that belonged to the allegorical addresses, so that their date remains still uncertain (P. Kahle in *ThLZ*, 82, 1957, p. 644; J. T. Milik *Ten Years of Discovery in the Wilderness of Judaea*, London, 1959, p. 33 f.).

[1] Cf. Kümmel, *Verheissung und Erfüllung*, note 109; Moore, Judaism, II, p. 334 ff.; *Str-B.*, I, p. 486 f.

[2] Cf. E. J. Tinsley in *Interpretation, A Journal of Bible and Theology*, 1953, p. 421 f.

[3] Cf. p. 120, also *Didache* 9.1 and especially Dodd, *Fourth Gospel*, p. 411.

[4] For more than three hundred years Israel had lived in the midst of a Hellenistic world and that this had left its traces also in Israel is shown not only by the Qumran texts but also by archaeological evidence (E. R. Goodenough, *Jewish Symbols in the Greco-Roman Period*, I, 1953, p. 52, cf. also Davies, *Paul and Rabbinic Judaism*, p. 5 ff.). For the following section cf. p. 123 f.

Hellenist uses rather terms of space when thinking of the unity of the whole cosmos in God, of heaven and earth or of a nation. In ancient Israelite thought too, of course, there are beginnings which make the adoption of such thoughts possible. An individual like Achan can determine the fate of the whole nation (Josh. 7; II Sam. 21.5 f.; Deut. 13.13 ff.; 21 1 ff.; 25.5 ff.;). The group experiences itself as a unity, as a corporate personality.[1] In this way the two patterns are mixed. The ancient concept of the father of the tribe is still alive. Israel is proud of Abraham and is convinced that in him its fate has been decided long ago. It is the elect nation 'in Abraham' (Matt. 3.9; John 8.39; Rom. 9.6 ff.). But the new speculations attach themselves more to the patriarchs, Jacob and Adam. In the tradition which lies behind John 1.51 the Son of man replaces Jacob-Israel.[2] He is the new patriarch, the new Israel. Late Jewish speculations put Jacob-Israel as a heavenly figure above all angels.[3] That they go back to the time of the formation of John 1.51 is proved by Philo (*Confus. ling.* 146–8) who identifies the patriarch Jacob-Israel with both the divine logos and the first man made in the image of God. The latter view leads to the universalistic Pauline concept that Jesus is the patriarch of a new mankind, the 'last Adam' (Rom. 5.12 ff.; I Cor. 15.21 ff., 45). Adam however is the most suitable character because he, though originally regarded as the father of the race, became more and more a mythical figure which was increasingly identified with the figure of the '*Urmensch*', the 'first' or 'original man'.[4] In this way the conception of Indo-Iranian origin, that the whole cosmos is contained in the 'first man' is combined with the Semitic view that the destiny of the generations to come is contained in Adam. What Hellenism says in respect of the cosmos is now applied to Israel or mankind, just as can also be shown to have happened with

[1]H. W. Robinson, 'The Hebrew Conception of Corporate Personality', *ZAW, Beiheft* 66, Berlin, 1936, p. 44 ff.

[2]C. K. Barrett, *The Gospel according to St. John*, New York, 1955, p. 156. If Psalm 80.16 (p. 45) really is the origin of the concept in John 15.1 ff., this stems from a Son of man tradition also.

[3]So the apocryphal prayer of Joseph quoted in Origen, *in evang. Joh.* 2.31 (25), cf. *comm. in Gen.* 3.12(19) = Migne 12, p. 81.

[4]Originally these are two distinct conceptions (J. Duchesne-Guillemin, *Ormudz et Ahriman*, Paris, 1953, p. 78); cf. p. 120 ff.

other concepts.[1] What was there meant in a cosmological sense receives a soteriological application in later Judaism.[2]

From there it is only one step to the statements on the true Vine in which all the branches, or the Body of Christ in which all the members are contained. In an entirely different terminology the same idea that we find in Paul is to be found in John, though they are entirely independent of one another. This in itself refutes the suggestion of an underlying fully developed Gnostic *saviour* myth. Certainly, mythical views of the 'first man', within whom the whole cosmos is contained, have become very prevalent. But the 'first man' is no saviour. Therefore the fact that the earthly Jesus has gone the way of humiliation to ultimate exaltation as the fulfilment of the way of Israel, and that he called disciples to follow him, that is, to share this way with him, has resulted in the application to Jesus of a pattern of thought familiar at the time. In this connexion the idea that all Israel could be represented before God by one individual is fundamental. John 15.1 ff. regards Jesus as the true Vine, that is to say the true Israel, and Paul regards the body of Christ as the Israel of God, the Church, the *kahal Jahveh* (cf. Gal. 6.16 etc.). The Hebrew conception of time is not the same as ours.[3] We should never forget that the Hebrew verb has no tenses. An event of the past is 'present' for those whose life is founded on it. Thus the salvation of Israel from the Red Sea is a *present* event for every generation in Israel (Amos 3.1[4]). On the other hand an event which is contemporary according to an abstract mathematical time conception may be quite meaningless for someone who does not know about it, and

[1]G. Schrenk, *Th.Wb.* V, p. 978: In Judaism the Hellenistic conception of God as the Father of the cosmos is changed into the conception of God as the Father of the people of the Covenant. M. Dibelius—H. Greeven, *Kolosser, Epheser, Philemon (Handbuch z.N.T.)*, Tübingen, 1953, p. 79 on Eph. 4.5: the Hellenistic formula of unity which places side by side *one* God and *one* cosmos receives an ecclesiastical form already in Judaism. The *one* temple now becomes the parallel to the *one* God.

[2]A different conception again is that Jesus is representative of *God* (E. L. Allen, 'Representative Christology in the New Testament', in *Harvard T.R.*, 1953, p. 161 ff.).

[3]Cf. Th. Boman, *Das hebräische Denken im Vergleich mit dem griechischen*, 2nd edition, Göttingen, 1954, p. 104 ff.

[4]Cf. the famous sentence in the paschal liturgy which says that man in every generation is obliged to regard himself as if he had left Egypt (Pes. 10.5; *Str-B.* IV, 68).

is therefore not 'present' for him. In this sense the body of Christ crucified and risen is present for every believer; the true Vine is present every day when the Church receives all her strength from this Jesus who some ten or two thousand years ago has walked with his disciples through Palestine and has been crucified and exalted for them. Therefore the true Vine as well as the body of Christ describes the 'area' where the blessings and the dominion of Jesus Christ are still present for the believer, the 'area of the church'.[1]

Thereby Paul, according to Gal. 3.16, begins by thinking entirely within the Jewish conception of the promises given to Abraham and his descendants. By a curious rabbinical exegesis he first of all proves that these were applicable not to a great number but only to one individual who represents the whole offspring of Abraham, just as with the prophets the 'remnant' represents the whole of the nation. Jesus alone is '*the* seed of Abraham'. But at the end of the same chapter Paul declares: '*Ye* are Abraham's seed' (Gal. 3.29). He can only say this because for him the ancient thought of the prophets, which represents in one individual the people elected by God, is as a matter of course combined with the much more 'modern' concept that this individual contains all the others within himself and that he mediates to them the divine blessing that rests upon himself. All those who have been baptized are 'in Christ' and they are all 'one man' in him (Gal. 3.28).

But even more important is a second observation: according to John 15.1 ff. the 'branches' are one with the 'Vine' in that they, the disciples, go the same way as he himself went, hated by the world, obedient to the Father, until after their earthly death he will exalt them in his glory. And similarly with Paul the unity of the members with the body consists above all in the fact that they 'carry the death of Jesus in their body', because they, as he himself, are persecuted, exposed to humiliation and suffering until they also share with Jesus in his exaltation to the glory of the Father.[2]

[1]This becomes even more understandable if one remembers the characteristic meaning of time in the Revelation of Saint John, according to which what is yet to happen on earth has already taken place in heaven. The same is expressed in Judaism by the conceptions of the pre-existence of the Law, the tabernacle, the Messiah, etc.

[2]The σὺν Ἰησοῦ therefore is always also the σὺν ὑμῖν (II Cor. 4.14; 7.3). Cf. p. 91, 112.

V

JESUS AS THE SUFFERING AND EXALTED SERVANT OF GOD

A SECOND amazing fact can be explained in the light of the conception of the suffering and exalted Righteous One, namely the remarkable use in the NT of the title 'Servant of God'.[1] This also is an expression which at first was applied to Israel, then to individual people such as the patriarchs or David, and eventually, especially in later Judaism, to the righteous in general. Within the words of God 'the righteous one' may already refer to the Messiah as the second David in Ezek. 34.23 f.; 37.24 f.; Zech. 3.8. However it is no pre-Christian *title* of the Messiah. As far as we can gather from the available material the aspects of suffering, especially in Isa. 53, are neither in the OT nor in pre-Christian Judaism applied to the Messiah. The LXX interprets Isa. 53 in a collective sense and applies it to Israel.

The findings in the NT are very remarkable. On the one hand it is obvious that the expression was applied to Jesus at a very early date (perhaps even by himself). On the other hand it is equally clear that the idea of atoning suffering has played only a minor part in this. The expression 'Servant of God' itself is found only in two passages, namely once in Matt. 12.18 and four times

[1]That Jesus regarded himself as the suffering Servant of God of Isa. 53 is the opinion of J. W. Bowman, *The Intention of Jesus*, Philadelphia, 1943, passim (esp. ch. III); essentially the same view is expressed, albeit somewhat more guardedly, by A. Oepke, *Th.Wb.* I, p. 536, J. Jeremias, op. cit. V, p. 698 ff.; V. Taylor, *Mark*, p. 618 f.; L. S. Thornton in K. E. Kirk, *The Apostolic Ministry*, London, 1946, p. 71 ff.; H. W. Wolff, *Jes. 53 im Urchristentum*, 1950 (crit. by E. Käsemann, *VuF*, 1948–50, p. 200 ff.) cf. also Maurer, *ZThK*, 1953, p.1 ff.; Knox, *Acts*, p. 72 ff.; Taylor, *Mark*, p. 445, and *Names of Jesus*, p. 36 f. The opposite view is expressed by R. Bultmann, *Theologische Rundschau*, 1937, p. 26 ff.; C. T. Craig, *Journal of Religion*, 1944, p. 240 ff.; also K. G. Kuhn, *ThLZ*, 1950, p. 406 ff.; Ph. Vielhauer, *VuF*, 1951–2, p. 35. Cf. more recently: Cullmann, *Christology*, p. 60 ff.; C. Lindhagen, 'The Servant of the Lord', *Exp. Times*, 1955–6, pp. 279 ff., 300 ff.

in Acts 3 f. Neither passage makes any reference to his passion. Acts 3.13 is reminiscent of Isa. 53 but refers primarily to his exaltation, and in 4.27, 30 Jesus is regarded as parallel to David the servant of God (v. 25, cf. Didache 9.2 f.; 10.2 f.).

Likewise the quotations from Isa. 53 occurring in the NT are never connected with his atoning passion. Apart from the use for apologetic purposes of Isa. 53.12 in Luke 22.37 ('he was reckoned with transgressors') only Acts 8.32 f. deals with the passion of Jesus. But here too only his silent suffering and the ensuing deliverance by God are emphasized. Even Matt. 8.17 regards the phrase 'he himself took our infirmities and bare our diseases' as realized in Jesus' miracles of *healing*! The other passages (Matt. 12.18 ff.; John 12.38; Rom. 10.16; 15.21) give various kinds of allusions.

One should however add those passages which are reminiscent of Isa. 53 though without direct quotation. We then find the idea of vicarious suffering or propitiation first of all in the pre-Pauline form 'who was delivered up for our trespasses' (Rom. 4.25). Mark 10.45 ('to give his life a ransom for many') can hardly be regarded as a word of Jesus, because the idea of atonement is absent from the parallel in Luke, but could be comparatively old. The same can be said even more emphatically of Mark 14.24, though, as far as I can see, the thought of his death 'for many' does not belong to the earliest form of the words of the institution but only the idea of the Covenant.[1] Finally I Peter 2.21–25 presupposes the idea of propitiation, though in its context the passage is used only as an example for the obedient suffering of slaves.[2]

The conclusion seems to me to be obvious. At an early date the descriptions of the Servant of God have been used as a description of the way of Jesus. As in later Judaism all innocent suffering was regarded as atoning, often vicariously for all Israel,[3] this con-

---

[1]Cf. E. Schweizer, 'Herrenmahl', *ThLZ*, 1954, p. 580 ff.; article 'Abendmahl im N.T.' in *R.G.G.* I, pp. 12–17, for Mark 10.45 Barrett, *N.T. Essays*, p. 1 ff.

[2]Other passages cited by Jeremias, *Th.Wb.* V, p. 707 f. are not convincing: παραδιδόναι (I Cor. 11.23 ff.; Rom. 8.32) is very frequent, with εἰς χεῖρας (Mark 9.31; 14.41) often in LXX but not in Isa. 53; with εἰς θάνατον (Isa. 53.12) in II Cor. 4.11 it refers to the apostle, not to Jesus; ὑπέρ is not found in Isa. 53; ἐντυγχάνειν (Rom. 8.34) is far more obvious in the case of Moses and the martyrs than in Isa. 53.

[3]Cf. p. 25 f.

cept was easily implied. But it did not become effective immediately just because it was so obvious.[1] It was just not suitable to express the uniqueness of Jesus. Jesus was called the Servant of God because every righteous one who took on himself suffering and humiliation for God's sake was so called.[2] If the uniqueness of this particular Servant of God was to be emphasized, that which distinguished him from the many others, then he would have to be described as the One who went this way at the end of Time, in fulfilment of all things. Then he would have to be described as the One in whom was fulfilled all that the Scripture said of all the servants of God. He would then have to be regarded as the promised second David, as the Servant of God of the last days. Even so this implies that his atoning work is final, that it is the concluding and comprehensive atonement. This is the beginning of an extremely important development.

We have already found that at first the narrative of the Passion was told without any explanation of this suffering. It was described in the words of the Psalms of suffering; it was emphasized that according to God's will this was how it had to be. This was the same necessity that was decisive for the passion of Israel and of the righteous in Israel, who voluntarily accepted God's decree which led them to humiliation and suffering.

Already in the words of Mark 14.24 and 10.45 which we quoted before, the death of Jesus has been placed at the centre. Consequently the idea of vicarious suffering and the ransom metaphor must become important. But the language of sacrificial worship also had its influence. Even before Paul the Church spoke of the 'blood of Jesus' that had been poured out. Very little blood is actually shed with a crucifixion. At this point, therefore, the language is influenced not so much by the historical death of Jesus as by the attempt to understand his death in terms of the familiar sacrificial worship. This holds good of Mark 14.24, also of the expression 'propitiation by his blood' which is not usual with Paul and which he probably borrowed from the language of

[1]Therefore only a few passages in the Gospels could be cited in which the idea of the atonement appears *expressis verbis* (only Mark 10.45; 14.24; John 1.29). It is entirely absent from Peter's addresses and from formulas like Rom. 1.3 f.; Phil. 2.6–11; I Tim. 3.16.

[2]Cf. also H. J. Cadbury, in *The Beginnings of Christianity*, ed. F. J. Foakes Jackson and K. Lake, 1/5, London, 1933, p. 364 ff.

the Church (Rom. 3.25), and finally of John 1.29.[1] This brings us to the formulation of the faith of the Church, which Paul borrows from her:

> 'Christ died for our sins, according to the Scriptures;
> and he was buried;
> and he hath been raised on the third day, according to the Scriptures;
> and he appeared to Cephas; then to the Twelve.' (I Cor. 15.3–5[2])

The two saving events of his death and resurrection are here placed parallel to one another, both emphatically regarded as fulfilment of the Scriptures and both supplied with an explanatory postscript. They are endorsed the one by a reference to his burial, the other by a mentioning of the appearances. It is emphasized that they are 'eschatological' events, that is to say events which conclude God's history as recorded in the Scriptures and bring it to its fulfilment, and also that these events are guaranteed by witnesses.

But what is the actual content of this fulfilment? Paul uses the formula in the context of his epistle above all in order to speak of the resurrection of Jesus. But in itself it puts the main emphasis on the death of Jesus. For it contains the emphatic assertion that this death took place 'for our sins'. Therefore what benefits the Church is his death in the first place. The resurrection of Jesus is the divine endorsement of this, the showing forth of God's 'yes' to this deed.

Along the same lines is the formula for the Lord's Supper, I Cor. 11.23 ff., adopted by Paul, which in substance at least, according to his opinion, has also come from Jesus himself.

---

[1] Cf. p. 34, n. 6.

[2] The extent of the quotation cannot be ascertained with certainty. V. 8 certainly is Paul's own. Here he speaks in the first person of his own calling. But neither, of course, does the inserted remark v. 6b belong to the old formula. As the construction of the sentence breaks off in v. 6, and vv. 3–5 form a unit which is complete in itself and consists of two parallel groups of statements, the quotation probably does not exceed these three verses. That Paul borrowed the phraseology from the tradition as well is shown by the non-Pauline expressions ἁμαρτίαι (plural), κατὰ τὰς γραφάς, ὤφθη, ἐγήγερται, οἱ δώδεκα (J. Jeremias, *Die Abendmahlsworte Jesu*, Zürich, 1949, p. 96, Engl. tr. *The Eucharistic Words of Jesus* by A. Ehrhardt, Oxford, 1955, p. 129 f. Cf. also E. Lohse, *Märtyrer und Gottesknecht*, pp. 113–16; and W. Baird, 'What is the Kerygma?', *JBL*, 76, 1957, pp. 181–91).

Certainly, here in particular it becomes clear that the idea of the Covenant is probably the most ancient interpretation of this meal. But this covenant is fulfilled in the death of Jesus and the addition of 'for you' to the phrase 'this is my body' underlines the vicarious meaning of this death.[1]

It is the great significance of Paul that he has so firmly adopted this line. With him it has become so central that at times he can even say that he has nothing to proclaim save Jesus Christ and him crucified (I Cor. 2.2; cf. Gal. 6.14). Paul is a trained theologian. He realized that the message concerning Christ remains exposed to all kinds of naturalistic, sacramental, moralist or even just sentimental misinterpretations as long as it has not been made unmistakably clear how the way of Jesus has a place in the forefront of the Church and how it works for her good. This is not a new development. For when we examined the words about 'discipleship' we noticed the outstanding pre-eminence of Jesus' way, his calling and his actions in relation to the disciple's. It could never occur to anyone that the way of a disciple was on the same level with that of Jesus. For they had all been taken by him on *his* way; they all merely shared *his* way.

But Paul has not merely *emphasized* this; he has also defined it more precisely. What the Church had already expressed in the figurative language of sacrificial worship or in commercial terms he has formulated in legal terminology. Legal language is more precise and less exposed to misinterpretation than the language of religion or commerce. By the proposition of the justification of the believer by grace, not in virtue of merit, Paul has grasped the decisive point. In this connexion the particular manner of Jesus' death has also become important to him. Crucifixion is a manner of death which is under God's curse. The dishonour, the humiliation of Jesus has here become complete: vicariously and atoning for the Church Jesus has become a curse (Gal. 3.13). This asserts the pre-eminence of Jesus' way in relation to the Church's more sharply than it is done anywhere else. There is hardly one of the NT writings which does not hold to this 'for us'. In all that we shall still have to say this should not be overlooked. Without the emphasis on this everything else would be wrong. That Paul has

---

[1]Cf. R. Schreiber, *Der neue Bund im Spätjudentum und Urchristentum*, thesis Tübingen, 1955 (*ThLZ* 1956, p. 695 ff.).

made this unmistakably clear gives his epistles their great importance within the NT.

We have thereby found the point of origin on the one hand of the discourse on the vine and the branches or the body and the members, and on the other hand of the doctrine of the atoning death of Jesus in the early Christian view of the suffering and exaltation of Jesus.

We can summarize: one can distinguish thus between four conceptions of representation:

(*a*) The Representative is the end of history: its meaning is fulfilled in him.

(*b*) He is the father of the race: he has already determined the destiny of the succeeding generations.

(*c*) He is an 'inclusive personality': a great number is included in him as water is contained in a vessel.

(*d*) He is the one who acts vicariously: a multitude is delivered by him because he does or suffers what all ought to have done or suffered.[1]

(*a*) and (*b*) think in terms of a temporal scheme which includes successive generations in history. (*c*) and (*d*) think in terms of a local scheme which includes quantities, the one and the many, which exist separately but at the same time. As long as the question remains purely Christological it is sufficient to say (*a*): Jesus is the end, the eschatological fulfilment of Israel's history. But as soon as one begins to think of the essence of the Church (*b*) seems to be obvious. This however could not mean physical generation, and the succeeding generations of the later history of the Church could not be conceived of as long as the end of the world was expected soon. Consequently the father concept appears only in the late Jewish form in which Adam, not Abraham is the father (Rom. 5.12 ff.). But Adam is no longer the father in a merely biological sense but as a mythical personality. 'In Adam' therefore can be understood in complete analogy with 'in Christ' (I Cor. 15.22) according to the conception (*c*). An event of the past is in the Hebrew conception of time present for those who are living under the blessings issuing from it, and under the dominion which it still exercises over their lives. Therefore the scheme (*d*)

---

[1] Conversely the many can be burdened by the injustice of one (Josh. 7.1; Rom. 5.12).

has a clear influence and can appear in combination with (*c*)
(II Cor. 5.14 f.).[1] But both conceptions receive clear correction by
the fact that Jesus had called men to follow him. It is true that
following Jesus in suffering and love is not a merit, not a condition for a man's being included 'in Christ' or his being allowed to
regard his work as done for him. But fellowship with Christ can
apparently take no other form than that Christ takes those who
follow him with him in his way. We shall now have to examine
the further development of this view.

[1]Strictly speaking those to whom v. 15 applies have been delivered from
the very 'dying' of which v. 14 speaks. The fact that the two assertions are
linked together guards against the two extremes which were rejected on
p. 11.

VI

JESUS AS THE ONE WHO WAS EXALTED TO BE THE 'LORD'

(The early Church; Rom. 1.3 f.; I Peter 3.18; I Tim. 3.16)

THE death and resurrection of Jesus are the two events which more than anything else have determined the early Church. In the development which we have just pictured the main emphasis was on his death. But we have started from the supposition that the Easter event was the decisive fact. The Church regarded this as the exaltation of Jesus to God's right hand. Peter's sermons in Acts still show a preaching in which the death of Jesus was regarded merely as a gateway to his exaltation and this alone was important. His death is not yet regarded as a clause of the creed. It serves merely as an accusation of the hearers. What then did this exaltation mean to the Church?

It seems to me to be clear that already the Aramaic-speaking Church worshipped Jesus as the Lord.[1] For the Aramaic formula *maranatha* has in this form been adopted by the Greek-speaking Church (I Cor. 16.22; cf. Rev. 22.20; Didache 10.6, Copt. text). Ps. 110 which speaks of the 'Lord' sitting at the Lord's right hand is the most frequently quoted passage of the OT. But these often quoted arguments can be supplemented by a whole series of others. Reference to the faithful as those 'who call on the name of the Lord' is widespread,[2] and Matt. 7.21 f. also shows that already in the early Church Jesus was invoked as 'Lord'. The same can be said of the primitive wording of Acts 2.36 which shows the influence of Ps. 2.2. In such a central pre-Pauline passage as

[1]Cf. W. Bousset, *Kyrios Christos*, Göttingen, 1913; *Jesus der Herr*, Göttingen, 1916; W. Foerster, *Th.Wb.* III, p. 1038 ff.; Fuller, *The Mission and Achievement of Jesus*, p. 111 ff. In opposition to Bousset: F. Filson, *The New Testament against its Environment*, London, 1950, p. 36 ff.

[2]I Cor. 1.2 (Ps. 98.6; Joel 2.32); cf. II Tim. 2.22; Acts 9.14, 21; 22.16; James 2.7; Herm. sim. VIII, 6.4.

Phil. 2.11 the title has not been borrowed from the Hellenistic conception of a saviour but from the OT. Moreover we know from II Cor. 12.2 ff. that at the end of the 'thirties Paul already accepted the guidance of the exalted Christ, and from Gal. 1.16, as well as from what we can find in the Acts, that his encounter before the gates of Damascus was a meeting with the Exalted One.[1]

But apart from the title its *content* can be traced elsewhere as well. If the expectation of the coming of the Son of man with the clouds of heaven was primarily the expectation of the vindication of Jesus by his exaltation to the right hand of God,[2] then the early Church simply acknowledged that this had been fulfilled by the ascension of Jesus. The disciples' meeting with the risen Lord led them to establish themselves in Jerusalem with their families and make him known to all people. From the very beginning therefore Jesus as the exalted One has determined their course just as the earthly Jesus had done before his death. The whole of the first period is firmly stamped with prophetic guidance. But the Spirit which ruled the Church was the Spirit sent by the exalted Lord. And if we may draw conclusions from what little we know of this guidance by the prophets, then the Church regarded the instructions of the Spirit as the instructions of the risen Lord. At any rate to the prophet of Rev. chs. 2–3 the words 'the Spirit saith to the Churches' (2.7 etc.) are identical with 'these things saith he that holdeth the seven stars in his right hand' (2.1 and many similar expressions), and in the Acts of the Apostles references to guidance by the Spirit alternate with those to guidance by the Lord. Moreover the Church cast out demons and healed the sick 'in the name of Jesus'; she baptized 'into the name of Jesus' and so placed the person baptized under his dominion. All this makes it very unlikely that they regarded the exalted Lord as waiting inactively in heaven.[3] This too has no prototype in the Hellenistic

[1] Cf. also Acts 7.56 (cf. p. 41, note 1); the development from Mark 13.35 into Matt. 24.42 (ὑμῶν!) and the lengthening of the address Rabbi =κύριε in Matt. 15.22; 20.30 f.; also 25.37, 44. Cf. p. 78, n. 2.

[2] Cf. p. 39, notes 3, 4, and the references there.

[3] This does not exclude the possibility that the latter view may *also* have arisen at a very early stage or in certain sections of the early Church in which the apocalyptic expectation of the near *parousia* was particularly strong. To a very great extent, we shall have to reckon with very different influences alongside one another. But at all events this does not hold good of the whole

belief in the *kyrios*.[1]

But in which sense then was Jesus the Lord? Dalman already stated that the definitive use of the expression 'the Lord' was impossible for the Aramaic-speaking Church. This Church regarded Jesus as '*her* Lord', the Lord of the body of disciples, the Lord of the Israel of the latter days.[2] For all that we have said so far describes the relationship of the Church to her Lord. He guides and guards her and she obediently serves him. This naturally implies that this Lord is stronger than all other powers which arise against the Church, stronger than Herod and Pilate and the Jewish Sanhedrin which persecute her (Acts 4.24 ff.). But the decisive assertion is that Jesus is *her* Lord, the Lord of the Church.

The passage, Rom. 1.3 f., which we have already discussed, also belongs to this stage. Here the death of Jesus is not even mentioned. The most important event is the appointment of Jesus

of the early Palestinian Church. Acts 3.21 probably represents a case of application to Jesus of an expectation of Elijah (O. Bauernfeind, *Die Apostelgeschichte, Th. Handkommentar zum N.T.*, Leipzig, 1939, p. 66 ff.). I cannot agree with the view expressed in J. A. T. Robinson's article in *JThSt* n.s. 7, 1956, p. 177 ff., that the whole of Acts 3.12–26 is more or less old tradition. It is a typical Lukan composition with some old phrases which he took over from liturgical material. Cf. v. 12: ἄνδρες Ἰσραηλῖται = 2.22; 5.35—τί θαυμάζετε = correction of a misunderstanding as in 14.15, also 2.15, v. 13: Old Testament quotation at the beginning of a speech as in 2.17–21, cf. 17.24a; 13.17–25. vv. 13b, 14; reproach as in 2.23; 13.27–29, v. 15: ἀρχηγός: 5.31, cf. 2.23 f., 36b; 4.10 (the relative clause is verbally the same!); 5.30; 10.39 f.; 13.29 f. The last clause is almost verbally identical with 2.32, cf. 5.32, v. 16 is not possible without the context. For v. 17, cf. 13.27; 17.30, v. 18: διὰ στόματος as in Luke 1.70; Acts 1.16; 4.25; 15.7—πάντες οἱ προφῆται as in 10.43, cf. Luke 24.27, v. 18b, is Lukan also according to Dr Robinson, v. 19: μετανοεῖν καὶ ἐπιστρέφειν is typical Lukan language, cf. 26.20 (both verbs often). v. 21b = Luke 1.70. For v. 25, cf. 2.39, v. 26: πρῶτον at least is only possible at a time where the mission to the heathen was already going on. That the view expressed in vv. 20, 21a is one of the most primitive christologies is none the less true. In Judaism one can compare the dominion of the Messiah over his people before the beginning of the Kingdom of God; of the Son of man in Enoch and IV Ezra; of the angels and archangels, especially 'prince' Michael. More details in *Erniedrigung und Erhöhung*, par. 11c.

[1]Cf. already Bousset, p. 148 ff.

[2]That the Greek text has ὁ κύριος as a rule is not surprising. The Aramaic *rabbi* too is rendered ὁ διδάσκαλος and the only possible Jewish address 'my (our) brother' regularly appears as ἀδελφοί without μου in the writings of Paul. It is entirely absent from Eph., Col. and the Pastoral epistles but is frequent elsewhere in all the epistles of undoubted Pauline authorship.

as the Son of God on the occasion of his resurrection, that is to say, his exaltation. His life on earth is depicted as the life of the Son of David. This may simply have been taken over from official Jewish theology. For this expects an Israelite king of the line of David to reign on earth as the Messiah. But surely the historical reality of Jesus' life in no way conforms to this expectation. Therefore we must ask at least if the expectation of the Davidic servant of God[1] has not had a decisive influence here. At all events the earthly existence of the Son of David has clearly been regarded as the lowly first stage which was fulfilled only by exaltation to the Sonship of God.

The interesting point about this passage is that the two stages are characterized by the ideas of 'flesh' and 'Spirit'. They denote the earthly sphere to which applies what was said in the first phrase, and the heavenly sphere in which the consummated Sonship of God has become a reality.[2] This is the contrast which we find in Isa. 31.3. Human eyes can see only the first, but he who has been granted the privilege of seeing with God's eyes can behold the second.[3] Even the idea that Jesus has been *appointed* the Son of God originates in Jewish, not in Hellenistic thought. Above all, however, we are here confronted with a very primitive Christology which regards the exaltation as the first beginning of Jesus' Sonship of God. This is important because we find here at a very early stage the beginnings of a formula that later became extremely prominent in the Hellenistic world. The same division into an event in the terrestrial sphere of the flesh and one in the heavenly sphere of the Spirit appears again in I Peter 3.18 (cf. 4.6) and especially in I Tim. 3.16. It was to become particularly fruitful for the Hellenists. For they primarily think in terms of spatial distinction between the divine world above in the heavens and the world possessed of all possible powers below on the earth, and not as the Jew thinks in terms of a temporal distinction

---

[1] Cf. p. 49.

[2] κατὰ πνεῦμα cannot be understood in an instrumental sense as this would be impossible in connexion with κατὰ σάρκα. The same holds good of I Tim. 3.16. For the Jewish background of the distinction, cf. the author's article in *Th.Wb.* on δάρς.

[3] Cf. the motivation of this in E. Schweizer, 'Röm. 1.3 f. und der Gegensatz von Fleisch und Geist vor und bei Paulus', *EvTh*, 15 (1955), p. 563 ff.; *Th.Wb.*, article σάρξ.

between the present evil age and the divine age to come.[1] To the Hellenist therefore the real problem is the union of heaven and earth, not the replacement of the old by the new age. The conception of the exaltation of the righteous One to God in his world above is then the starting point for an assertion which above all thinks in terms of this spatial formula.

[1]Both ways of thinking are already mixed in Judaism of NT times (cf. Gal. 4.25 f.). The same is true of the Jewish concept of the Ascension as the final vindication of Jesus. Cf. also p. 45 f., 123.

VII

JESUS AS THE ONE WHO WAS HUMILIATED FROM DIVINE GLORY AND EXALTED TO DIVINE GLORY

(Phil. 2.6–11; I Tim. 3.16; Col. 1.15–20; I Peter 3.18–22)

BEFORE we discuss the language found in these passages we shall have to examine the hymn quoted by Paul, Phil. 2.6–11.[1] He praises Christ who, 'being in the form of God, counted it not a thing to be grasped to be on equality with God, but emptied himself, taking the form of a servant, being made in the likeness of men; and being found in fashion as a man, he humbled himself, becoming obedient even unto death, yea the death of the cross. Wherefore also God highly exalted him, and gave unto him the name which is above every name; that in the name of Jesus every knee should bow, of things in heaven and things on earth and things under the earth, and that every tongue should confess that Jesus Christ is Lord, to the glory of God the Father.' The first stanza which speaks of the humiliation of Jesus reaches its climax in the words 'obedient even unto death'. It is probably Paul himself who, interpreting, adds the thought important to

[1] There is no doubt that the passage has the character of a hymn; it is however possible that Paul himself turned to this style, as he did e.g. I Cor. 13 or Rom. 11.33 ff., or reverts to a hymn which he had made on another occasion (L. Cerfaux, *Miscellanea historica in honorem Alberti de Meyer*, 1946, I, p. 122). But since E. Lohmeyer's analysis ('Kyrios Jesus', *SAH*, 1927–8) nearly all scholars agree that we are dealing here with a pre-Pauline hymn to Christ in two or three stanzas. This is made probable not only by a vocabulary that is unusual for Paul (μορφὴ θεοῦ, ἴσα θεῷ, δοῦλος, κενοῦν, ὑψοῦν, χαρίζεσθαι, used of Christ), theological thoughts which are foreign to him and the absence of assertions which otherwise are of central importance to him, but apart from the hymnic form, above all by the fact that the statements made here are quite unexpected in the context of the epistle. Nowhere else in the writings of Paul can he be found to put together a long series of Christological assertions without being led to this by the context. For the exegesis cf. E. Käsemann, 'Kritische Analyse von Phil. 2.5–11', *ZThK*, 1950, p. 313 ff.

him 'yea the death of the cross'. In the old text death is simply the last stage of obedience. The meaning of obedience in this passage is: acceptance of suffering. And this is explicitly indicated by the concept that we find so frequently in the OT and in Judaism: it is 'humbling himself'. This is indeed the expression of his real humanity, his appearance as a man. But here this humiliation of his in obedient suffering to some extent reaches backwards. It has a preliminary stage. For that he came 'in the likeness of men' is not a matter of course. This is already self-humiliation, acceptance of the form of a servant. Here, however, extremely difficult questions of interpretation arise. The expression 'form' ($\mu o\rho\varphi\acute{\eta}$) does not mean either the mere outward manifestation, so that the reference was only to a 'change in the appearance of the godhead', or the substance, so that an actual change of the essence was spoken of, but the *status*, the 'state, the position, the place'. For it is interpreted by the statement that its bearer relinquished 'the form of God' because he 'regarded it not a thing to be held fast, to be on equality with God'.[1] What interests us above all is the term 'servant', which like the word 'obedience' brings us back to the world of ideas connected with the suffering righteous one. This is the concept which specifically denotes the godly man who knows that he is obliged to render obedience to God. For the acceptance of the form of a servant is here described as an entry into a relationship of obedience unto death, and the statement 'he counted it not a thing to be held fast' signifies that the resolve to humble himself was a conscious decision of the pre-existent Christ, an act of obedience. Accordingly the exaltation is regarded as a reward for this obedience, and the end appears as universal obedience to God by the confession of Jesus as 'Lord'. Here we find a Church in which mankind finds its fulfilment in obedience, in which such obedience is as a matter of course realized in humiliation even unto death. It should however be noted that this death in itself has no special significance in relation to salvation, but is merely the deepest stage of this humiliation, followed by exaltation, because the obedience has reached its climax in this death. This is the Church determined by the Old Testament and Judaism, in which real humanity means obedience, service, being a servant,

[1]The discussion with the exegetical literature can be found in *Erniedrigung und Erhöhung*, 6g.

and in which real humanity finds its fulfilment only in a consciously positive attitude to this position.

One should however not think of *the* Servant of God, as Lohmeyer does. For this would not necessarily mean that Jesus became a 'man', but that he became the one foretold by the prophets. His oneness with man would then, it is true, be implied, but the *emphasis* would be on his uniqueness by which he was distinguished from all men. But neither does Käsemann's interpretation, that by his humiliation Jesus became a slave of the powers of nature in the Hellenistic sense, commend itself. In either case a genitive would have had to be added: servant of God, or servant of the powers of nature. So the 'form of a servant' simply denotes his state of humiliation as contrasted to the 'form of God'. But this designation is only true in a context in which, in the way already described, human existence is essentially understood as such service. It is, of course, possible that Hellenistic Churches thought of man's slavery under the powers of nature. But, as the emphasis on obedience shows, originally the reference was to the ancient conception of the man who, as an obedient sufferer, is a servant before God.

The second stanza is linked by the characteristic word 'exalt'. By the word 'wherefore' this is explicitly presented as the consequence, indeed as the reward of the suffered passion. Here, as in Rom. 1.4, the exaltation consists in an appointment to a new dignity which results in the granting of a new name. This is the name of *Kyrios*, Lord. This includes the worship of all the forces and powers throughout the whole expansion of the cosmos, from heaven, around the earth, right down to the underworld. Unfortunately it remains uncertain whether this worship is regarded as already taking place or as something belonging to the future.[1] If the latter is the case then this would be a survival of the view that Christ is reigning from the ascension till all is subject to him.[2]

[1]Especially if in v. 11 one reads the *subj. aor.* However both readings allow of both interpretations, for in the active and middle the future tense is little more than a specialized form of the *subj. aor.* Paul probably understood the saying in the first sense, but this means nothing as regards the preceding stage (cf. I Peter 3.22 and F. W. Beare, *The First Epistle of Peter*, Oxford, 1947, p. 150 f.).

[2]Cf. J. A. T. Robinson's expression 'inaugurated eschatology' (*Jesus and his coming*, p. 101 f.).

Here two points of the further development should be noted. The assertion of the self-humiliation of the Servant of God under the suffering imposed by God, has received entirely fresh force by its extension to the act of the pre-existent Christ, and at the same time the assertion of Jesus' lordship over his Church has been extended to a dominion over the whole of the cosmos. Both points have genuine beginnings in early statements of the primitive Church. A disciple who was called by Jesus to follow him had already met God himself in this calling. This was the case in particular when Jesus called a publican or when he sat at table with publicans. The earliest Church has attempted to express this by saying that God 'had sent' Jesus, that Jesus 'had come'. And she has left no doubt that she regarded this mission and this coming as something unique, unparalleled in any other mission or any other coming. Speaking of the mission and the coming of the One who was equal to God, Phil. 2.6 f. has expressed this in such a manner that only one interpretation was possible.[1] But even Jesus' lordship over the Church, as we saw, naturally implied for her that he was Lord over all the other forces and powers. Otherwise she would not have been capable of meeting suffering and death for her Lord as confidently as she did. This certainty is here also expressed unmistakably and comprehensively. Yet it cannot be denied that in these two points we are dealing with a new formula, the significance of which we shall examine later on pages 100 ff.

First however we follow the development of the statements on the humiliation and exaltation of Jesus. The same theme that we found in Rom. 1.3 f. is also present in the first two parts of the hymn, I Tim. 3.16. Here the content of the creed is:

> 'He, who was manifested in the flesh,
> justified in the Spirit,
> seen of angels,
> preached among the nations,
> believed on in the world,
> received up in glory.'

Here too the death of Jesus is not emphasized, indeed is not even referred to. The development already observed in Phil. 2.6 f. has

[1]Cf. p. 101 f.

here continued still further. His earthly life is described very briefly as an epiphany in the flesh. But contrary to passages like I Cor. 15.3 this earthly existence as such is already an object of confession of faith. It is already a miracle in its own right. It does not become this only in virtue of the added interpretation 'for our sins' (I Cor. 15.3). But the emphasis of the hymn is on the exaltation.

The two spheres are clearly presented in a local sense as the two halves of the cosmos, one above the other. It is true that this depends on the interpretation of the hymn. But it should be clear that the lines are joined together in an inverted order so that every time an event 'below' and an event 'above' appear together in pairs.[1] But how is exaltation understood here? Jesus is 'justified', proved to be righteous by it. This is also the oldest view according to which the Easter events meant the justification of Jesus' way, his vindication. They proved that Jesus was the 'Righteous One'. The idea is that of a lawsuit between God and the world, as it is often found in the OT. Not the world, the sinner, is the accused but God or his Messiah who is accused and rejected by the world.[2]

But how does this justification come about? The following four stages describe the triumphal procession of the exalted One through the terrestrial and celestial spaces. 'Seen of angels' describes his triumphal procession, ascending to heaven, while angels worship him. According to the fourth and fifth lines the same happens on earth: 'preached among the nations, believed on in the world.' Even the nations which have so far lived in heathen enmity towards God, worship him. The logical conclusion is formed by the taking up of Jesus into the glory of the Father: 'received up in glory'. This is remarkable because we are wont to regard the exaltation of Jesus to the right hand of God as the presupposition for the beginning of his continuing mission. Perhaps the position at the end of the hymn goes back to an ancient formulation in which exaltation, presentation (before the circle of

---

[1] That is to say the scheme is ab-ba-ab. Cf. the argumentation in *Th.Wb.* VI, pp. 414.26 ff. Discussion of the literature in *Erniedrigung und Erhöhung*, 7d.

[2] ἐδικαιώθη must be interpreted in the light of Rom. 3.4 (=Ps. 51.6), where the verb is placed parallel to νικᾶν. It is obvious that originally this conception was at home only in Jewish thought (cf. Ps. Sal. 2.16; 3.5; 4.9; 8.7) and simply means the entry into the divine sphere.

the gods) and enthronement (as the seizure of power) follow one another. Such patterns are known in Egyptian enthronement ceremonies.[1] For that reason alone one should not attach too much importance to this order. More relevant however is the observation that the formation of the creed has reached a further development. We no longer find a strictly chronological order of the successive saving events. The two first lines summarize the work of salvation as a whole; the two next lines maintain that the act of salvation and the proclamation of the gospel belong together;[2] and finally by the last two lines the singing Church praises the victory of the Saviour in logical (not chronological) order. Here the important point is only that heaven and earth have become one again.

Here too it is very clear how the ancient message of the lordship of the exalted One has germinated. Here even more than in Phil. 2.9–11 it is emphasized that his dominion is so all-embracing that it has welded heaven and earth together again. The main interest of this Church is evidently focused on this.

The same can be said of the hymn in Col. 1.15–20.[3] Here a new point is that the subjection of the cosmos to Jesus is based on the fact that all things were created 'in him'. Yet the reconciliation of all things with God, the atonement, that is to say the reunion of heaven and earth, has first come about through the saving work of Christ. In the present text v. 20 mentions the blood of his cross, which is very strange by the side of 'through him' which is probably original. As the fresh start in v. 18b, which is parallel to the beginning of v. 15, unmistakably refers to the resurrection from

---

[1] J. Jeremias, *Die Briefe an Timotheus und Titus* (*Das neue Testament deutsch*), Göttingen, 1949, p. 21. The traditional order is slightly different: hymn of the heavenly beings (not here)—guidance (3–5 ?)—surrender to the judgment (2) —deification, access to God (6) as collected and abundantly demonstrated by J. A. Festugière, *La révélation d'Hermès Trismégiste*, III, Paris, 1953, p. 149 ff.

[2] Cf. Luke 24.47; Acts 2.32; 3.15; 5.32; 10.41; 13.31; I Cor. 15.3–5; II Cor. 5.18 f. And H. Conzelmann in M. Dibelius, *Die Pastoralbriefe* (*Handbuch*), Tübingen, 1955³, p. 51.

[3] On this question cf. E. Käsemann, *Eine urchristliche Festliturgie*, *Festschrift R. Bultmann*, Stuttgart, 1947 p. 133 ff.; Ch. Masson, *RThPh*, 1948, p. 138 ff.; E. Percy, *ZNW*, 43, 1950–1, p. 183 ff.; R. Leivestad, *Christ the Conqueror*, London, 1954, p. 97 ff.; Chr. Maurer, 'Die Begründung der Herrschaft Christi über die Mächte nach Kolosser 1. 15-20', in *Wort und Dienst, Jahrbuch der theol. Schule Bethel*, 1955, p. 79-93; also N. A. Dahl. *JBL* 76, 1957, p. 270 ff., Studia Theologica, c.ord.th. Scandinavicorum ed., I, 1948, p. 77, 81 f.

death which made Jesus the 'firstborn' and the 'preeminent' (πρωτεύων) it seems likely that originally the hymn regarded this as the reconciliation of all things with God. The addition 'through the blood of his cross' by a Pauline emphasis on the cross as the act of atonement has afterwards guarded this statement against the Gnostic misinterpretation that this was a purely physical act of salvation. The middle part (vv. 17, 18a) which extols Jesus as the Head of the Church—regardless of whether it does or does not belong to the original hymn—shows the influence of the confession to Jesus as the Lord of the Church and to the Body of Christ. What at first was expressed by a cosmic form of speech is here really tied up with what the Church has always recognized in Jesus Christ. Ideas which were originally cosmological are thereby moulded into a soteriological form.[1] In Phil. 2.6–11 and I Tim. 3.16 the mere fact that she sings this praise is sufficient to show that the Church is the community of those who know about his dominion and therefore share in it. Here the Church is explicitly described as the body whose Head is the Lord of all things. Here too the decisive declaration of faith is the union of heaven and earth again achieved by him.

Finally we would refer to I Peter 3.18–22. First of all in v. 18 ('put to death in the flesh, but quickened in the spirit') a formula appears which reminds one of that in Rom. 1.3 f.; I Tim. 3.16. Even the expression in v. 22 'who is on the right hand of God, having gone into heaven' is certainly a formula. Perhaps the passage is based on a complete hymn.[2] At any event in v. 22 the exaltation of Jesus is the goal of the confession. This is interpreted by the end of v. 22: 'angels and authorities and powers being made subject unto him.' Here the subjection of all powers is unmistakably represented as having already taken place. There are also various reasons for assuming that the preaching to the spirits in v. 19 was originally held to have taken place on the occasion of the ascension, that is to say in the region between heaven and earth where, according to the Hellenistic view, the realm of the spirits is to be found. This means that in this section we have reached a stage that is thoroughly influenced by Hellenistic thought.

[1]Cf. p. 47, n.1.
[2]Thus R. Bultmann, *Coniectanea Neotestamentica* XI, 1947, p. 1 ff.

VIII

JESUS AS THE ONE OBEDIENT IN SUFFERING AND THEREFORE EXALTED TO THE FATHER

(The Gospel according to John, the Epistle to the Hebrews)

THE ultimate effect of the confession of the suffering and exalted Righteous One has however been far greater. In the Gospel according to John and the Epistle to the Hebrews it has its effect not merely on some isolated formulas but on the whole christology. The picture of Christ in the Fourth Gospel is entirely determined by the idea of obedience. The Father-Son relationship is shown by the fact that Jesus offers obedience and the Father rejoices in this (John 10.17). Jesus keeps his Father's commandments (John 15.10). As the Father taught him he always does the things that are pleasing to him (8.28 f.), not his own will but the will of him that sent him (6.38). He keeps *his* word (8.55); he speaks nothing from himself, but the Father gives him the commandment (12.49). Indeed he can do nothing of himself but what he sees the Father doing (5.19). Therefore his food is to do the will of him that sent him and to accomplish his work (4.34).[1] In a specially emphasized passage, on the eve of his death, Jesus is represented as the One who renders the services of a slave,[2] and this is explicitly shown to be in an inevitable tension with the name 'Lord' with which the disciples address Jesus—address him as the Lord with full right, for so he is (13.13 f.).

---

[1]Cf. also ch. 5.30, 36; 7.18, 28; 13.14; 17.4; the emphasis on his seeking only the Father's honour (8.49 f.) and on the fact that all things have been given to him by the Father (3.27, 35; 5.22, 26 f.; 7.16; 8.28; 12.49; 13.3), his permanent communion with the Father through the Spirit (1.33; 3.34) and the angels (1.51), his being one with the Father (10.30) but also his constant attention to his 'hour' (2.4; 7.6; 13.1; 17.1).

[2]Washing the feet is about the only thing one cannot even let a Hebrew slave do, but only a foreign slave (*Str-B*. II, p. 557).

That here the death on the cross is the end and the completion of this obedience is again unmistakable. The commandment that he has received from the Father is that he shall lay down his life in order to receive it again. The Father loves him because he does this (10.17). Jesus' loving 'to the end' finds its expression in the passion (13.1). He takes the road to the cross so that the world may know that he does as the Father has commanded him (14.31). And again it is clear that here his death has no merit of its own in the sense of propitiation.[1]

Equally frequent in the Gospel according to John is the reference to Jesus' exaltation or glorification.[2] In 17.4 f. Jesus prays: 'I glorified thee on the earth, having accomplished the work which thou hast given me to do. And now, O Father, glorify thou me with thine own self with the glory which I had with thee before the world was.' This thought has however assumed a very characteristic form here. The close connexion between the deepest humiliation and exaltation, which in the above petition could still be thought of in terms of obedience and reward, is here presented in such a fundamental way that to John it is in the very death of Jesus in absolute obedience that complete union with the will of the Father is already present, so that the exaltation itself takes place in this death. There is no doubt also that according to 8.28 and 12.32 f. the crucifixion itself is the exaltation. The remarkable double meaning of the word ὑψόω plays a part here, as this can refer both to the outward 'being lifted' on the cross and to the exaltation to new glory. Ch. 6.62 has also probably a double meaning in a similar sense; however much Jesus' 'ascending' is to the believers the fulfilment of his way, to the world it is only a stumbling-block, because the world can see only the death of a condemned person. Here too Jesus' death is merely the final consequence of his way. That is why even before Jesus' death his exaltation can be referred to in the past *and* in the future tense (3.13; 12.28; 13.31 f.).

There is no reference here to the new name or the new dignity granted to the exalted Christ. There is no longer any need for it. For to John Jesus from the very beginning is the *Logos*, who is with God and who is God and who during his life on earth never

---

[1]Cf. only 1.29 (p. 34, n.6).
[2]The two expressions are connected also in Isa. 52.13; Ps. 37.20; 112.9.

in the least relinquishes his full oneness with the Father. As he always was and ever remained the Son, he cannot be appointed as the Son. To John the obedience which he renders as the Incarnate is nothing other than the expression of his absolute oneness with the Father. There can be no more mentioning of a new dignity.

And yet John speaks with emphasis of the exaltation. On the one hand this is the rendering of this whole, absolute obedience as it was completed on the cross; and on the other hand, conceived in a remarkable unity with this, his home-coming to the Father, the preparation of the mansions, the return to the glory which the Son had before the creation of the world (14.2; 17.5, 24), and which is no longer subject to the dialectic characteristic of all earthly obedience, in which exaltation must take place in humiliation.

If we compare this with the conclusions of the previous section then we should remember that the Fourth Gospel is preceded by the Prologue. Behind all references to the humiliation and the obedience of Christ is the thesis of the pre-existent One who was made flesh.[1] Humiliation and obedience therefore have the importance which is given them in Phil. 2.6 f. and I Tim. 3.16. Yet it must be maintained that Jesus' humiliation is still clearly presented in the old pattern of earthly obedience under humiliation and suffering. The concepts of the prologue are no longer explicitly used. The same can be said about the exaltation. This is certainly regarded as comprehensively as in the hymns we have quoted. Because of this event the ruler of this world has already been cast down, the last judgment has already taken place (12.31). But again this exaltation is conceived entirely within the old pattern of the 'reward' of the Righteous One. This dominion is not based on some mythical victory over demoniacal powers. It is already a reality in the absolute obedience of him who suffered and died. Thus all possibility of misunderstanding is avoided as if it were a question of a mythical act understood in natural categories,

---

[1]σάρξ, it is true, does not imply the sinfulness of mankind as in the epistles of Paul. Therefore incarnation in itself does not mean much more than: appearance in the sphere below. But this is done in obedience to the will of God, an obedience unto the cross, which is contrary to the behaviour of the world ruled by the devil (ch. 8.42–44). Cf. the author's article σάρξ in *Th.Wb.*

which just checkmated the enemy. By the absolute obedience of Jesus on the cross heaven and earth have been made one, and that is why all other powers and forces have been deposed. That is also why John can take up the idea of the lamb of God that taketh away the sins of the world and probably even understand the death of Jesus as the death of the Paschal lamb.[1] For it is in this absolutely obedient dying of the Man raised on the cross that this oneness has again been achieved. This is what Paul calls reconciliation. This is an event which is valid for the whole world and for all times.

Finally reference should be made to the Epistle to the Hebrews. Here his passion is characteristic of Jesus. The agony in Gethsemane with its 'strong crying and tears' (Heb. 5.7), but also the voluntary choice of the 'shame' of the cross (Heb. 12.2), and the 'reproach' therein contained (Heb. 13.13), are essential to the author. In such suffering Jesus was 'faithful' to his Creator, as Moses was faithful (Heb. 3.2, 5). He thereby 'learned obedience' (Heb. 5.8). Consequently the OT saying, 'Lo, I come to do thy will' is transferred to Jesus and regarded as fulfilled by his sacrifice on the cross (Heb. 10.9 f.). So here also the meaning of the whole earthly life of Jesus is seen again in that it is an obedient life, indeed in that this life represents consummate obedience.[2] Again such obedience shows itself in suffering which is regarded as humiliation and shame. Again we are right inside the conception of the suffering righteous one of Judaism.

Here also the act of humiliation is extended backwards into pre-existence. The text 'Lo, I come to do thy will', which we have just quoted, is applied to the advent of the pre-existent Christ from heaven (Heb. 10.5–10). This conception is also well represented elsewhere in the Epistle. Right at the beginning of the Epistle Jesus is referred to as the Mediator of creation, indeed as the Creator (Heb. 1.10). Only for a little while was he made lower than the angels (Heb. 2.9; see RV margin). Likewise in Heb. 5.7 the 'days of his flesh' appear to be merely an episode of his life from everlasting to everlasting. Consequently the incarnation is explicitly substantiated by his having to become equal in every respect to those whom he was to help. (Heb. 2.17 f.; 4.15; 5.2).

[1] Cf. p. 34, n. 6.
[2] τελειωθείς ch. 5.9; διὰ παθημάτων τελειῶσαι 2.10.

In this connexion special emphasis is put on his resisting the temptations.

Here however we have to inquire if the death of Jesus has not acquired an independent importance. No doubt in sacrificial language he is described as the unique sacrifice which sanctifies the Church (Heb. 7.27; 9.14 f., 26, 28; 10.12). But this concept—which is certainly central to the author—has been fitted into a scheme that actually follows a different pattern. Though in Heb. 2.14 it is said that Jesus partook of flesh and blood so that through death he might bring to nought him that had the power of death, yet in Heb. 5.7–9 the only reference is to his learning obedience in Gethsemane while his death (and his ascension) are indicated merely by the expression 'being made perfect'. That is to say, it was regarded as the final, finishing stage of his obedient suffering which had begun with his humiliation to human existence. Here his death on the cross is substituted for his earthly life of obedience as a whole, without any change as regards the content. This holds good also of the passages where his death simply means 'shame', rejection by men, humiliation (Heb. 12.2; 13.12 f.). But, above all, the doctrine of the sanctifying sacrifice on the cross is fitted into a scheme of thought in which the going up to heaven is the really important event. In the Epistle to the Hebrews this going up to heaven corresponds to the High Priest's going into the Sanctuary. This however cannot be done without a sacrifice. Thus the sacrifice on the cross opens to the new High Priest the way to heaven. Strictly speaking the cross is therefore not the saving event itself, but the act that makes the saving event possible.[1] This by no means implies that to the author the cross was of secondary importance; the very fact that he fits it into a scheme that originally did not mention it in this form shows how important it is to him, and in other passages it can also be shown how the cross has a correcting influence on the text. But at bottom there is a way of

[1] According to 9. 14 f. the death of Jesus is the cause of the redemption of the transgressions; according to 9. 16 f. the condition for the coming into force of the testament (which is an argumentation without much prospect, as in this case the testator certainly does not die); but according to v. 18 ff. it corresponds with the sprinkled blood by which God's Covenant with men is effected. This only shows that there is no question of a consistent theory of atonement here.

thinking which regards the whole earthly life of Jesus as an act of obedience which is above all completed in his shameful, humiliating passion.

But here again we find the conception that the exaltation is the reward or at least the necessary consequence of the obedience in suffering: Because he suffered death 'Jesus has been crowned with glory and honour' (Heb. 2.9). Already in Heb. 1.9 the quotation from the OT stated that God has anointed him because of his righteousness.[1] In Heb. 5.5–10, also, the exaltation follows immediately after the obedience of Jesus by which he was 'made perfect'. The two are probably much more closely connected than the traditional exegesis allows. For if one admits[2] that the prayer of Jesus which was heard by God was no other than one for his exaltation from his death (which was to follow), then it becomes clear that the whole passage is meant to demonstrate only that the exaltation of Jesus was a just exaltation based on the obedience rendered by him and not an assumed dignity (5.4!). Then the parallel with John 12.28 and with the early conception of the ascension as the vindication of Jesus becomes obvious.

And also the assertion that Jesus receives a new name which gives him a new dignity is found here again. There has certainly been a considerable development. Thus it is maintained that from eternity Jesus is the effulgence of God's glory and the very image of his substance (Heb. 1.3). Yet the unique position of Jesus is not the natural result of his divine nature but something won by struggle. It is said that he has become by so much better than the angels because he has inherited a more excellent *name* than they have (Heb. 1.4). Here just as in Acts 13.33 (and the original form, Rom. 1.4) Ps. 2.7 is applied to the exaltation of Jesus (Heb. 1.5; probably also 5.5),[3] although the author certainly could not say in the strict sense of the word that the begetting of the Son takes

---

[1] The same is stated in ch. 12.2 if this is to be rendered 'for the sake of the joy that was set before him' (Windisch, *Hebräer*, p. 109 f.; Michel, *Hebräer*, p. 293 f.); if it means 'instead of the joy' then the thought is similar to that in Phil. 2.6 ff.

[2] Here I agree with J. Jeremias, *ZNW*, 44, 1952–3, p. 107 ff., another view is expressed by C. Spicq, *L'épitre aux Hébreux*, 1952–3, II, p. 114 ff.

[3] Thus also E. Käsemann, *Das wandernde Gottesvolk*, 1939, p. 58; H. Strathmann, *Der Brief an die Hebräer* (*Das NT deutsch*), Göttingen, 1949, p. 73 thinks of the baptism in Jordan.

place at this 'day', of the ascension. The dignity to which the ascended Christ is appointed is strictly speaking no longer that of the Son but that of the High Priest of the order of Melchizedek, as is stated by a quotation from Ps. 110.4 which seems to be connected with Ps. 2.7 (Heb. 5.5 f.). Here for the first time appear together these two psalms which have become of such importance in the presentation of the idea of exaltation. Heb. 5.9 shows that the appointment as High Priest is a consequence of the obedience rendered (also cf. Heb. 2.17).

The acceptance of this new dignity means that Jesus 'sits down on the right hand of God'. In Heb. 1.13 this is supported by Ps. 110, and this is repeated four times in Heb. 1.3; 8.1; 10.12 f.; 12.2. The idea is the same as in Acts 2.33 f.; 5.31; I Peter 3.22; but similarly in Mark 12.36; 14.62 par.; 16.19; Rom. 8.34; Eph. 1.20; Col. 3.1; often with reference to Ps. 110 which however is probably at the root of all these passages even where it is not directly mentioned. According to Heb. 10.12 f.; 12.2 the accession to the throne at the right hand of God follows immediately after the death on the cross.[1] The resurrection is not referred to anywhere. Only Heb. 13.20 may come near this, if the alternative reading 'from the earth' given by some ancient authorities is not the oldest.

But above all the ascension itself becomes important here. The significance of Jesus can be summarized by saying that he has 'passed through the heavens' (Heb. 4.14). Heb. 9.11–28 also speaks of this. However here the decisive fact is his appearance before the throne of God in order to make intercession for the Church. The analogy of the earthly high priest who only after making a sacrifice dares to pass through the veil of the temple and to appear before God, makes it possible for the author to fit in the idea of Jesus' self-sacrifice on the cross which he regards as essential.[2] Heb. 6.20

---

[1] According to ch. 9.11 ff. also the entry into the sanctuary, that is to say the ascension to heaven, follows immediately after the offering of the blood of Jesus on Good Friday (J. Jeremias, *ZNW*, 42, 1949, p. 198).

[2] Cf. p. 72. If it is recognized how great the influence of this analogy is here, then one must ask, whether this really is an 'ascent to heaven' in the proper sense of the word; that is to say whether this must be seen against the background of the mythological conception of the ascent of the saviour through the many-storied heavens. Josephus describes the 'veil' between the porch and the holy place which was 'of the same size' (as the second 'veil' before the Holy of holies) in these words: 'It was to be a model of the

also affirms that Jesus is the Forerunner in that he has become a High Priest by entering into that which is behind the veil.[1]

Thus the exaltation is here understood as an ascension which means the beginning of Jesus' intercession for his Church before the throne of God (cf. Rom. 8.34).

Thereby we have completed the cycle in which the idea of Jesus' humiliation and exaltation has been decisive. It should be added that this conception also affects Paul even though with him it is not right at the centre. Yet he too discloses that he regards the coming of Jesus into the world as self-humiliation: 'The grace of our Lord Jesus Christ' consists in 'that, though he was rich, yet for your sakes he became poor, that ye through his poverty might become rich' (II Cor. 8.9). He too knows of the 'obedience' of Jesus (Rom. 5.19). But Jesus' Lordship is to him of central importance. 'Jesus is Lord' can be a summary of all that the believer confesses (I Cor. 12.3). But this confession of Jesus as the Lord is identical with the confession of his resurrection (Rom. 10.9). Here also this is primarily understood as his exaltation. Indeed Paul can so state this, that the only purpose of the saving events, of the death and the resurrection of Jesus, is this his being the Lord of the living and the dead (Rom. 14.9). Moreover Rom. 8.34 declares that the fact of the resurrection of Jesus is even 'more' than the fact of his death, because it implies his sitting at God's right hand and his intercession for his Church. That Jesus is the Lord implies for Paul too the subjection of all other powers. According to I Cor. 15.25 f. this comes about step by step until the *parousia*; but passages like Rom. 8.38 f.; I Cor. 8.6; Gal. 4.8 show that in principle these powers have already been vanquished.

---

universe. The tapistry gave a picture of the whole heavens with the exception of the zodiac,' and says of the Holy of holies: 'This was separated from the holy place similarly by a "veil"' (b. 5. 207 ff.) Doubtless this pattern of the veil and even more any possible interpretations of these pictures originate in cosmological speculations. But even if our passage had been influenced by such speculations and not by any knowledge of the pattern of the veil itself, it would scarcely be based on the myth of the ascension of a saviour but rather on Stoic speculations of the logos pervading the universe, linked with the Christian conception of Jesus' exaltation to God's right hand.

[1] Cf. W. Manson, *The Epistle to the Hebrews*, 1951, p. 57 f. and the influence of these texts on I Clement 36.

This is definitely stated in Col. 2.15:[1] all principalities and powers are made to walk as prisoners of war in the triumphal procession of Christ (which was probably assumed to have taken place at the ascension).

[1] I more and more doubt that Paul could be the author. Apart from the arguments usually levelled against his authorship there is the observation made on p. 58, n. 2.

IX

DISCIPLESHIP AFTER EASTER

(Revelation, St John's Gospel, the Epistle to the Hebrews)

WE have established that the death of Jesus at first made an end of the disciples following him. Discipleship can no longer have the form of a real walking with him. Thus the Church has never quite overcome her hesitation about extending the expression 'following Jesus' to the time after his death. Rev. 14.4 is the only passage where this has explicitly been done. This shows that the Church has been fully conscious of the uniqueness of Jesus' way. That is why the obvious solution, namely that of regarding the way of Jesus as the *example*, in a kind of timelessness, allowing of imitation by all generations at all times, has *not* been advanced. This solution would not be wrong, but rightly it occurs only on the fringe of the NT, where it is safeguarded by other assertions. But the *substance* of what was meant by 'following' remains alive, especially where the humiliation and exaltation of Jesus have also become important.

This is shown by the very fact that the Church has preserved the words referring to 'following Jesus'. She has not handed these words down as historical memories of a past period. She was convinced that they were very much alive and made an active appeal to those who heard them. This is already evident in the Synoptic Gospels. We saw that the connexion of the words on discipleship in Mark 8.34 ff. with the announcement of the passion in vv. 31–33 has followed in the course of tradition. That is to say, the Church has linked the suffering of a disciple with the passion of Jesus by the conception of discipleship in the sense of walking behind Jesus. This is not a chance editorial arrangement of Mark. For the same connexion appears in John 12.24–26 in a tradition which knows the saying on hating one's own life but which can hardly be attributed to Synoptic origins. Here too this saying is connected with a word on discipleship and with an announcement of

Jesus' death. It is therefore clear how far the Church has experienced her sharing in the way of Jesus exactly in terms of walking behind him on the same road of suffering and persecution.

This was already implied in a passage like Matt. 8.19 f. which promised the disciple that he would share the tribulations of Jesus. Here in particular it is clear that Matthew has regarded the life of the Church as a following of Jesus. He places these words on discipleship at the head of the miracle story of the stilling of the storm which he takes from Mark and introduces this explicitly by the note 'his disciples followed him.' Thus he gives this story a definite character picture of discipleship. That is to say he has already recognized in this little boat the Church and in the plight of the disciples the Church's destiny in her following of Jesus. To her too discipleship meant storm and billows but in the midst of those her being with the Lord who is able to still the wind and the waves.[2]

Finally the absolute use of the title of 'disciple', which probably originated in the early Church, shows how important this idea of discipleship was to her.

To appreciate the further development of the understanding of discipleship we start from the only passage where the word 'follow' does not refer to the relationship to the earthly Jesus. This runs: 'They were they which were not defiled with women; for they are virgins. These are they which follow the Lamb whithersoever he goeth. These were purchased from among men, to be the first fruits unto God and unto the Lamb' (Rev. 14.4.)

It has long been remarked how reminiscent this passage is of the Synoptic words on discipleship. This in itself makes it unlikely that 'following' here denotes the state of the blessed in heaven. In spite of the present tense the reference is to their following him on earth. Here the Lamb is still represented very realistically as the Leader.[3] The expression 'whithersoever he goeth' which is in complete agreement with the terminology of the words on discipleship (Matt. 8.19), shows that the reference is

[1]Cf. also W. Marxsen, *Der Evangelist Markus*, 1956, p. 128.

[2]G. Bornkamm in '*Wort und Dienst*', 1948, pp. 49–54. In Matthew also nobody but the disciples (except Judas) adores Jesus as the 'Lord' (cf. G. Bornkamm in *The Background of the N.T. and its Eschatology*, p. 250 f.).

[3]Cf. Rev. 7.17, but there referring to the life in heaven. This shows that following Jesus on earth is continued on a heavenly level in glory.

not simply to a mere imitation but to a real walking-behind. We should ask whether the present tense could be interpreted as a past: 'whithersoever he went', that is, on his earthly road to the passion and death and resurrection. But in view of Rev. 7.17 this is very improbable. Thus the idea probably is that the Lamb walks ahead of the believer on every turn of his way on earth.

What is new in these words therefore is that here the Exalted One is regarded as the One who precedes the follower. Fundamentally there is nothing new here. The Church which formulated Mark 8.34, or added the word on bearing the cross, or at least understood the expression, which Jesus had already used, in a new sense after Good Friday, had already essentially taken the same step. Indeed wherever the Church has preserved the words on following Jesus she has taken this step. It is hardly possible to be sure how far it was said that Jesus' way through humiliation to exaltation shows the way to his followers, and how far the conception of the exalted Lord, governing and guiding his Church in all her steps here and now, has been active. In most cases the two ideas have probably amalgamated, as seems to be suggested by the ambiguous wording of Rev. 14.4.

But other aspects of the old words on discipleship also recur in interesting variations. If in Jesus' words discipleship meant the exclusion of all other obligations, here freedom from all defilement by women is mentioned. Unfortunately we are not sure what this means. The passage would be particularly interesting if it referred to defilement by idolatry, adopting OT figurative language, as used again in Rev. 14.8 and probably also in Rev. 2.20. Then the individual demands of giving up boat or tax-desk, father or riches would be summarized in one demand: to relinquish all idolatry, to remain faithful to the one Lord and not to forsake him. The all-embracing demand of Jesus that one should surrender oneself, one's own life, would then have found its characteristic expression in a situation in which alien gods presented themselves as Jesus' competitors. But probably this is merely a warning against unchastity or even a recommendation of celibacy. Thus a general demand in a field that was of particular importance to the author may have been substituted for the differentiating individual demands which we meet in the life of Jesus.

From the beginning the calling of Jesus has been understood

as also being a calling of election, a calling of grace. This is asserted here with much emphasis and in the words of already familiar terminology: 'These were purchased for God and the Lamb.' That which became visible only in the contrast between Jesus and the unclean tax-gatherer or with man in general with no merit to his credit is now explicitly stated. The 'calling' which precedes the following is a 'purchase'. This is the statement of a Church which is already looking back to the passion of Jesus and recognizing in it the foundation of all the grace she has experienced.

Finally, it must be said that the promise of future glory, which often was only implicit in Jesus' words on discipleship, appears in a strongly marked form here. For in the vision of the apocalyptic author this goal has already been achieved (Rev. 14.1). But this glory is still regarded as sharing the destiny of the Lamb, as continued walking behind him (Rev. 7.17), indeed as sitting down with him in his throne (Rev. 3.21).[1] For strictly speaking the phrase no longer is a *call* to discipleship but a picture of the glory of those who have heard this call and have come to the end of their course.

In the Gospel according to St John we have to start from ch. 1.35 ff. where, as in the Synoptic Gospels, the calling of the disciples is described. Here the word 'follow' is repeatedly used with great emphasis (John 1.37, 38, 40, 43). That is to say this passage sets out to show in a characteristic way what discipleship is. Here too, in v. 43, the initiative comes from Jesus. But it is no accident that in the first example it is not Jesus himself but the Baptist, Jesus' witness, who mediates the calling by simply pointing to Jesus as the Lamb of God. This means that the important point is not that the earthly Jesus calls. The testimony to Jesus in itself is already a calling without any specific imperative being needed. Whether this testimony is given by the earthly Jesus or by his messenger makes no difference as far as the substance is concerned. In this testimony the pointing to the Lamb corresponds with what in the previous passage was meant by the purchase.

[1]The unity of the destiny of Jesus and that of the disciples becomes clear when we compare Rev. 1.5 and 2.13 ('the faithful witness'); 2.8 and 10; 2.26–28 and 12.5; 19.15; (22.16); also 21.7; 22.5.

Likewise the thought that discipleship implies the severance of other ties appears in a characteristic form. The first scene at once makes it particularly clear that here the issue is a severance of ties; but no longer from possessions and family. To John there is a far more decisive and inclusive severance: that is from other figures from which man expects salvation. The first two disciples leave John the Baptist in order to follow Jesus.[1] Similarly in v. 46 Nathanael has to abandon the dogmatic views he has so far held in order to 'come and see' who Jesus is. With John, following Jesus implies 'seeing' (John 1.46, 50 f.; cf. 39), the knowledge that Jesus is the Messiah (John 1.36, 41, 45). This too is the logical conclusion of what in the Synoptic Gospels remains unsaid behind the accounts. When Jesus called with such authority and when such unqualified obedience really did take place, then certainly some such 'seeing' did happen. But this was not yet put into words, and could not be put into words, because only discipleship itself could show who Jesus is. It is true that John, as is shown by John 1.50 f., has not overlooked this either; but, as is generally the case with John, the post-Easter knowledge has been projected even into the first encounters in a way entirely different from the Synoptic Gospels. In a sense it is already the Exalted One who is calling here.

That a real and concrete sharing in the life and destiny of Jesus is part of discipleship has not been forgotten here either. The disciple comes to Jesus and abides with him (John 1.39; also vv. 42, 46). And finally in this passage it becomes particularly noticeable that discipleship means service, more specifically the service of a witness (John 1.41, 45).

That John does not restrict discipleship to the disciples of the earthly Jesus is shown by ch. 8.12: 'I am the light of the world: he that followeth me shall not walk in the darkness.' The parallel text ch. 12.46 shows that he can just as well say: 'Whosoever believeth on me' will 'not abide in the darkness.' It is possible that the expression 'follow' puts more emphasis on the fact that the believer is entirely dependent on Jesus, that is to say, that revelation is not something that one can possess, that one can

---

[1] For the Fourth Gospel clearly contains polemics against those who regard John the Baptist as a Messianic figure (cf. 1.8, 19 ff.; 3.27 ff.); and for an opposite view, J. A. T. Robinson in *N.T.St.*, 4, 1958, p. 279, note 2.

hold in one's hands; but it is clear that such following of Jesus can become a reality to everyone and at all times.

The same holds good of John 10.4 f., 27 f., where Jesus speaks of the sheep following him. Here the concrete meaning of the word has only been maintained within the figure of speech, but it is obvious that in this way the attitude of the believers of all times towards Jesus has been described (cf., e.g., John 10.26). Again characteristic features appear. Those who follow obey the calling of Jesus (John 10.3 f., 27a). This calling implies that the sheep have to break with all other shepherds (John 10.5). Following implies that mutual knowing of one another which gives complete fellowship, in which the chief consideration of their being safely guarded is strongly stressed (John 10.4, 27 f.; cf. v. 14 f.).

New is here the thought that the sheep are his own (John 10.3 f., 26 f.) and that the calling does no more than make this original owner-relationship visible. Certainly already in the Synoptic Gospels the calling was God's free act of grace. While at the first calls it is said that Jesus 'saw' the disciples, in the case of the rich young ruler this is described as a deliberate 'looking upon him'. John 1.48 goes one step farther: 'Before Philip called thee, when thou wast under the fig tree, I saw thee.' The electing look of Jesus is placed before the encounter with the person elected, so that it is underlined that he was foreordained. Our present passage goes one step farther and comes close to the conception which we know from the Qumran Sect where the idea of predestination is at least very near. But we should also refer to passages in the OT, in which it is assumed that in virtue of sovereign election by God his people were his property right from the beginning and that this owner-relationship is continually actualized in God's calling: 'I have called thee by thy name; thou art mine' (Isa. 43.1). Moreover, even in the OT, this election is not simply confined to one particular nation. On the one hand God also calls Gentiles: Bileam, Cyrus. On the other hand not the whole of the nation of Israel are God's own people, but the seven thousand whom God had appointed not to bow their knees before Baal (I Kings 19.18; Rom. 9.6 ff.). In John, ch. 10, as well as in the OT, the idea of a predestination is at the outset corrected by the other statement, that Israel's belonging to God and the disciples' belonging to Jesus is based on the act of salvation: on the deliverance from Egypt, on the 'purchase' by the death of the 'Lamb of God' (Rev. 14.4; John 1.36; 10.11–14). The two assertions ensure the absolute pre-eminence of the calling of Jesus, already emphasized by the Synoptics.[1]

We pass on to John 21.18–22. This word is an exceptional case, inasmuch as here explicitly the Risen One, in John's Gospel that is to say the Exalted One, is speaking, though speaking as the One who appeared on earth. Here, according to John 21.19a, Peter has been given the forecast of his death. Consequently the call 'follow me' (v. 19b) already envisages his death as a witness, as a martyr. What the word of Jesus on the readiness to give up one's life implied as a possibility has here become a direct prediction. Yet the demand is fulfilled by Peter first of all actually walking behind Jesus. But, of course, this is now merely a symbol. Where should he go together with the Risen One? But that the story is told as it is demonstrates to what extent this realistic interpretation still survives, and above all that martyrdom by no means exhausts the concept of following. Discipleship, that is following Jesus, begins immediately after the calling of Jesus, and thus includes the whole of a disciple's life thereafter. Every single step follows 'behind Jesus'. This is underlined by the fact that the disciple whom Jesus loved also 'follows' Jesus (v. 20), though he will 'tarry' (v. 22) and not suffer the death of a martyr. Here therefore the actual walking behind Jesus has become an expression to describe a life which aims at obedience in every respect to the very nod of the Exalted One and which experiences this belonging to him particularly but not exclusively in the death as a witness.

John 13.36 ff. is far more difficult to interpret. First of all it is unmistakably emphasized that 'following Jesus' is not dependent on the free will of a disciple, but must be given to him. 'Thou canst not follow me now; but thou shalt follow afterwards.' What had been expressed by the character of grace in the calling of election is thereby underlined once more. The application of this truth is therefore not confined to the very first calling only; it

---

[1]For this special conception of the Church in John, cf. my essay in *N.T. Essays*, 1959, p. 230 ff., and my book, *Gemeinde und Gemeindeordnung*, Zürich, 1959, p. 105 ff.

holds good afterwards as well. It is also unmistakable that Peter then declares his readiness to follow Jesus even into martyrdom, and for this very reason must fail because such following is a gift, and not simply a human possibility. But what does the 'afterwards' mean? Is it referring to a strengthening of Peter's character, which some time will be achieved? Does it mean to establish that the appointed time of this gift rests with God alone? Does it mean to state a qualitative distinction between the present time and that other time in which he will be granted the gift of following Jesus? It is first of all certain that Peter by the question 'whither goest thou?' does not recognize the character of Jesus' departure. This is shown above all by the continuation of the discussion in John 14.4–7. He is still reckoning with a wandering upon earth, that in the worst case may imply the readiness to die, but that otherwise can be done by anyone who is not a cripple. Jesus however is speaking of a departure which, being the way to death, is at the same time the way to the Father, to that house which has many mansions (John 14.2). And when he has finished his work he will fetch his disciples to join him there (John 14.3). True it cannot be denied that the reference is *also* to Peter's death as a witness. For if the promise 'thou shalt follow afterwards' is followed by Peter's offer to follow Jesus even to death and the prediction of his denial, then it is hardly possible not to see that the promise applies to *this* form of following too, which however will be a pure gift and not a human possibility. For though from the very beginning Jesus' way in suffering and death was preceded by the promise of his exaltation, in John's Gospel this is the case to a much greater extent. Here his exaltation to the Father already takes place in his very passion and death.[1] Certainly right from the beginning a disciple who gave up his life was promised real life, but now the same tune is set to a different key. The decisive thing now is Jesus' way to the Father. Here above all, as John 14.1 ff. shows, the disciple will also accompany his Master. It is true that the word 'follow', which has a too definite character, is not explicitly used for this purpose. It is said that Jesus will come again and take them to himself; reference is made to the 'way' which they know, and which he himself is. The promise 'thou shalt follow afterwards' therefore must be

[1]Cf. p. 69.

regarded as primarily referring to a martyr's death. But certainly at the outset sharing the fate of Jesus was already implied in discipleship. In words like John 10.4 f., 27 f., this was stressed so much that it implied complete fellowship, consisting in intimate knowledge of one another. But here such walking behind Jesus has a new note, not only because it is characterized as a gift of grace and not as one's own achievement, but above all because since Jesus went this way as a way to death, it is no longer a going down into destruction, but a return home to the Father. This idea was present from the beginning. Going with Jesus had never been regarded as heading for catastrophe but always as going to meet that passion and death which were sure of God's promise. But as distinguished from those first words, it is now no longer said only that with Jesus the eschatological hour has come, in which God's promise is fulfilled to him, and to all those who are with him; it is said that only Jesus' going before them through death to the Father prepares the mansions, and the way to them, for his followers.

Here we are on the threshold of a new development. While originally discipleship, following Jesus, meant the way of the disciple on earth, leading to self-denial and suffering, perhaps indeed to death, but which had received the divine promise of exaltation to the true life; now a new view can be distinguished in which the way to divine glory becomes the decisive thing for which the earthly way is merely a pre-condition. If we follow this line of thought, then a new view of the fellowship between Jesus and his disciples must become central. Now it is no longer Jesus' way into suffering which is also the lot of his disciple who is prepared to share his fate; no longer the earthly way of the disciple in which the Exalted One goes before with his guidance, his demand and his comfort; but the way of the disciple who has already reached his earthly goal and is now allowed to ascend to the Father like his Master. A gnostic understanding of discipleship would have been reached as soon as this point alone were stressed.

John 12.23 ff. is even more interesting, because here the words on discipleship of Mark 8.34 f. (or Matt. 10.38 f.) are repeated in a Johannine version. The introductory phrase states that the hour of the glorification of the Son of man has come.[1] This glorification

[1] Cf. p. 38 ff. and in particular p. 39 f.

is effected by his death or through his death, as expressed by the metaphor of the grain of wheat. The metaphor has been used frequently but this shows even more clearly that its application here is something new: the meaning of death is that the grain of wheat does not remain alone but bears much fruit. This means that Jesus' death has been understood in its significance as creating the community of the Church.[1] But how does the Church come into being? The words on discipleship provide the answer. In John 12.25, a saying also to be found in Mark 8.35 (Matt. 10.39): 'He that loveth his life loseth it; and he that hateth his life in this world shall keep it unto eternal life' appears in conjunction with v. 26, a variant of Mark 8.34 (Matt. 10.38): 'If any man serve me, let him follow me; and where I am there shall also my servant be, if any man serve me, him will the Father honour.' The last phrase shows that v. 25, which one would at first apply to Jesus, has, quite as a matter of course, been extended to the disciples in the same sense in which it is applied to Jesus. This seems so self-evident that one can no longer even say whether a particular phrase refers to Jesus or to his disciples. It holds good for both because they have reached full communion. An all-embracing 'being where he is' has been granted to whosoever follows him. But one should not overlook that the same combination of the three sayings is already found in Mark 8.31, 34 f. That Jesus' death creates the Church, therefore, does not hold good, as in Gnosticism, just because through an original physical relationship between the Saviour and the saved all that happens to Jesus will also happen to the disciples, but because of this 'following' by which the disciple enters into a fellowship which consists in sharing Jesus' destiny. All that is new is the natural way in which this thought is regarded as a foregone conclusion.

One could ask if the words on following do not refer to the glorification itself, that is to say, to 'accompanying Jesus' in his ascension to the Father, so that the promise 'where I am there shall also my servant be' would be merely an explanation. But one should not overlook that 'following' is referred to in the imperative while the future tense is used only afterwards. On the other hand it must be said that in this promise, as well as in the following phrase on the glorification by the Father, the presup-

[1] Cf. p. 83, note 1.

position is indicated only by the word 'serve'. The word 'follow' therefore has a middle position. It certainly still indicates 'serving', that is to say, the attitude of a disciple upon earth who walks behind his Master step by step and is appointed by him to the service of witness (John 1.35 ff.). But John 8.12 and 10.4 f., 27 f. have already shown how the main emphasis is on the disciples' being guarded and supported by Jesus, which is not implied in the idea of service. Here, as in John 13.36 ff., it becomes clear that 'being where he is' does not cease at death but achieves its full consummation only then. One should certainly not confine the honouring by the Father to life after death. Just as the glorification of Jesus takes place already at the hour, indeed precisely at the hour of his obedience on the cross, so also the honouring of the disciples. But that 'being where he is' also and above all includes that glory of the Consummated One, that is shown by the parallels, John 14.3; 17.24.

Because such following is based on an act of obedience (which is always a gift of grace) and not on physical identity, and because it is 'service', the way of Jesus, including his exaltation, retains its uniqueness (John 3.13) and its pre-eminence to the way of his disciples.[1] This is stressed by John 12.27–31, and v. 32 makes it conclusively clear that to 'be where he is' is dependent on the Exalted One 'drawing' his own 'to himself'. That here too the reference is not to physical relationship, which in later Gnosticism effects such 'drawing', should be obvious from John 6.44 where the same expression is used of the Father,[2] while John 3.14 f. shows that the fellowship of the disciple with the exalted Lord is one of faith.

Thus the tone has clearly been moderated. While at first discipleship consisted in obedient walking with the earthly Jesus, or after Easter under the guidance of the Exalted One, to which the promise of future glory was attached, in the Gospel of St John

[1]Even the abiding in the vine, which is expressed in a picture completely according to nature, is effected by 'keeping his commandments' (John 15.10) 'having part in him' takes form in 'doing as he does' (ch. 13.8, 15).
[2]Cf. Jer. 38 (31).3: εἵλκυσά σε where this denotes God's loving drawing men to himself. In II Kingdoms (Sam.) 22.17 the rescue from danger is described by figurative speech; in IV Macc. 14.13; 15.11 it is used of a mother's love (cf. A. Oepke, *Th.Wb.* II, p. 500 f.). John 6.45 interprets this 'being drawn' as 'hearing, learning and going toward Jesus'.

following Jesus certainly still includes this, but contains above all
—certainly in substance, if not also in the use of the word 'follow'
—Jesus' going to the Father after his exaltation. While originally
a disciple was sure of the promise because he himself was present
at the eschatological hour of the end of the old and the beginning
of the new world, and was one of the followers of the Man who
brought about the change, and while afterwards a disciple received this promise for the faithfulness with which he followed
the Exalted One at every turn of his way; now in the Gospel
according to St John it is stated that the exaltation of the disciple
is possible only in virtue of the exaltation of Jesus. This is not a
new thought, for there had never been any question of any glory
other than that which one was to share with Jesus. But the pre-
eminence of Jesus' way, especially his way to heaven, has become
pregnant in an entirely new sense.

Finally we must refer to the Epistle to the Hebrews. The word
'follow' is absent here. But the substance appears in a characteristic
form when Jesus is introduced as the 'Pioneer' or Leader. We
begin with the passage Heb. 2.10 f. In Heb. 2.9 Jesus was referred
to as the One 'who hath been made for a little while lower than
the angels', 'because of the suffering of death crowned with
honour and glory.' V.10 continues: 'It became him, for whom are
all things, and through whom are all things, to bring many sons
unto glory, by making the "pioneer" of their salvation perfect
through sufferings' (or: 'to make him who brought many sons
unto glory, i.e. the pioneer of their salvation, perfect through
suffering'). As in the Synoptic Gospels the passion of Jesus is
explained by the divine 'must'. But here this means logical necessity, necessity of thought, and no longer the law of the eschatological moment. Above all Jesus appears here as the 'Leader' of
the many sons who are to receive glory. Admittedly this expression is much disputed. One could also translate 'Originator'
(*Urheber*, so the RV: 'author') or 'chief' ('captain', AV). In the
Epistle to the Hebrews the significance of Jesus includes all three
conceptions. He is the 'forerunner' (Heb. 6.20), the 'author' of
eternal salvation (Heb. 5.9) and the One to whom all things are
subjected (Heb. 2.8). It is therefore not easy to tell which meaning
is most important to the author and which meanings have merely
complementary relevance. In the context it may however be

regarded as obvious that Jesus' way through the humiliation of death to glory and honour, depicted in Heb. 2.9, is the way in which the saved follow. The continuation points in the same direction: 'Both he that sanctifieth and they that are sanctified are all of one: for which cause he is not ashamed to call them brethren.'

This brotherhood again is not the physical relationship of the Gnostic system. The One from whom all originate here is not Adam but God. As Jesus is *'the* Son', so they are, according to the OT use of the term, 'sons' in virtue of creation. And yet this Epistle in particular maintains the uniqueness of Jesus' sonship and even in this passage does not lose sight of it. The brotherhood comes into being only by the act of the 'Leader' who acknowledges them. But this is clear: in such brotherhood, established by him, he goes before them in the same way which they have to go. In the following vv. (2.14–18) his incarnation is based on his ability as the heavenly High Priest to help those who are being tempted precisely by what he himself has suffered. It deserves notice that bondage to the fear of death and not sin is mentioned as that from which the 'brethren' are to be saved.

In Heb. 4.14–16 we read: We therefore have 'a great high priest, who hath passed through the heavens, Jesus the Son of God.' Here the journey of Jesus through the heavens has become relevant in itself. No longer is it merely another expression of the exaltation; it has assumed an importance of its own. It has become the saving event proper. But how? The first answer will have to be: his journey through the heavens is the event by which the 'Pioneer' paves the way for those who follow him. But this has been interpreted by the two verses which follow. The necessary condition of this passing through the heavens is his humiliation upon earth, where he, made equal to man, endures all temptations. As its goal, comes into view the throne of grace where he, together with the Father, is presumably enthroned. But this means that it is not actually his passing through the heavens, which procures salvation, but his intercession for men before the Father. And this he is able to exercise because he has himself suffered all temptations.[1]

This is confirmed by Heb. 6.20 where Jesus is referred to as the 'forerunner for us'. In what does this 'being a forerunner'

[1]For this and for the next all. cf. p. 74 f.

89

consist? In his 'having become a high priest' and 'entering into that which is within the veil,' just as the earthly high priest goes there to make intercession for Israel.

No different is the case in Heb. 9.11–28, where the saving event proper is his entering 'once and for all into the holy place' (v. 12) which is not 'a holy place made with hands' but 'heaven itself' (v. 24). But again, strictly speaking, it is not this entering itself that procures salvation, but the intercession for men before God made possible by it.[1]

Finally in Heb. 12.2 Jesus, after the description of his way to the cross and up to the right hand of God, appears as the Pioneer and Perfecter of faith unto which the Church has to look in her temptation. Here the way of Jesus comes perhaps very near an example and the following of the Church near imitation. But with the passages, Heb. 2.10; 5.9; 6.20 one must not overlook that Jesus' work as the Forerunner has a basic character and does not only illustrate discipleship but is the only thing that makes discipleship possible. This becomes more obvious in Heb. 13.12 f. where following Jesus is described as going forth unto *him* who went without the gates of Jerusalem not only as the first One, but as the One who sanctified the people. Therefore it should be implied in the expression 'Pioneer and Perfecter' that *he* first creates the Church and that *he* perfects her.

Thus the Johannine beginnings have here been consistently thought out to their final consequences. The obedience of earthly life, it is true, is very important to the author. But Jesus is the 'Forerunner' and 'Pioneer' above all on the way from earth to heaven. That is why the fear of death is mentioned as the thing from which man has to be delivered. The common destiny of Jesus and his disciples in their earthly way through the temptations is shown by the fact that the Church knows that she is under-

---

[1] Cf. the discussion between W. M. F. Scott and H. Balmforth in *Theology*, 1953, p. 42 ff.; 171 ff.; 222 ff. Particularly ch. 10.10 ff. makes it clear that in Heb. the sacrifice is regarded as made once and for all and that, at least to the author, the intercession before God does not mean a continued sacrifice. After the sacrifice has been made the High Priest stands before God, making intercession (Scott, p. 47) so that at most he serves as the Mediator of the Church's sacrifice of praise (ch. 13.15, Scott, p. 48). A continued sacrifice in the Lord's Supper cannot be based on these words (Balmforth, p. 172). Therefore the parallels of Michael making sacrifice at the heavenly altar (Käsemann, *Das wandernde Gottesvolk*, p. 137) should not be too hastily cited.

stood by him who went the same way and who therefore can make intercession for her. Besides this way is her example, and in virtue of its ending in the sacrifice on the cross, it is also the foundation of her sanctification.

But the old conception of following Jesus is also to be found in *Paul*. For his fellowship with the Lord is most fulfilled in the persecution which the apostle suffers. He bears about in his body the 'dying of Jesus' (II Cor. 4.10). In this humiliation he is 'God's servant' and the 'stigmata of Jesus' which he bears branded on his body are probably scars left by scourgings (Gal. 6.17). His 'dying daily' takes place in persecutions and perils (I Cor. 15.31; Rom. 8.36). This does not at all correspond with the conceptions of the mystery religions, but is perfectly in accord with the sharing of a common fate into which Jesus receives his disciples.[1]

We will attempt to summarize briefly. The various themes of the Synoptic words on discipleship have had their characteristic development:

From the very beginning the *calling* of Jesus was essential. After Easter this call was issued by Jesus' witness (John 1.36). He could however look back on the completed work of Jesus and proclaim him as the Messiah. Therefore this knowledge is now found at the beginning of discipleship, even though it will grow to full maturity only during this discipleship (John 1.41, 45, 50 f.; the credal formulas of the Epistle to the Hebrews). Consequently those who follow Jesus are at the outset those who have been sanctified by the work of Jesus (Heb.), purchased by the Lamb (Rev.), who belong to him and are his own (John), whose sins have already been borne by the Lamb (John).

Their *service* is therefore described more precisely as the service of witness (John 1), which in certain circumstances also includes the death of a witness (John 13; 21; Rev.; Paul). This must prove true in the faithfulness which guards from apostasy (Heb.; also Rev.).

A great number of variations are found in the conception of *fellowship*, of sharing the same *destiny*. While at first this consisted

[1]This probably also explains Col. 1.24. By following Jesus an apostle shares in his way, not indeed in the sense that he would have to accomplish the act of salvation once more, but certainly in this sense, that his message is credible only if such following does take place. In this sense he suffers for the Church, as is expressly stated in II Cor. 1.4–7; 4.12, 15; 6.3–10.

in Jesus and his disciples going together to meet eschatological suffering, which would be followed by the glory of the Kingdom, after Easter the idea lived on as the guidance and protection of the Church by the Exalted One who was present in all difficulties and perplexities (Rev.; John 21). This finds a strong expression in the experience of being guarded (John 10) and of being understood (Heb.). But increasingly important becomes the idea that this does not cease at death, but continues on the way to heaven (John, Heb.), indeed in the blessed life in heaven (Rev.).

In all three spheres of thought Jesus has increasingly been regarded as the Saviour to whom those who follow owe their whole salvation. It is therefore understandable that the idea of abandoning all other obligations was not only stated in general terms (Jesus himself already speaks of giving up one's life, oneself; Rev.: fornication?) but was particularly formulated as a demand to relinquish all other saviours (John; perhaps Rev.; Hebrews also in connexion with the mere 'shadows' of OT worship).

X

THE UNITY OF THE CONFESSION OF CHRIST

WE will first of all examine the formulas which we have found in the course of our inquiry.[1] In these we meet the faith of the NT Church in a concentrated form. If then we ask first of all what they all have in common, then we must state a very simple and yet decisive fact: without exception they are all about Jesus Christ. Not one formula speaks of anything else but him, e.g. of the one God in contrast to the idols, or of the now living Holy Ghost, or of man and his destiny. All that does not appear till after the time

[1] A cursory glance at the *Apostolic Fathers* may at least show the course of the further development and how very different the credal forms here were from those mentioned so far. In the writings of Ignatius Jesus appears as 'God' (Ig. Eph. 18.2; Ig. Smyr. 1.1). Great importance is still attached to Jesus' being the son of David (Ig. Eph. 18.2; Ig. Tr. 9.1; Ig. Smyr. 1.1; disputed Barn. 12.10 f.; Ps. Clem. hom. 18.13), his conception by the Holy Spirit and birth from the Virgin Mary (Ig. Eph. 18.2; Ig. Tr. 9.1; Ig. Smyr. 1.1), the consecration of the baptismal water by the baptism of Jesus (Ig. Eph. 18.2), the reality of the incarnation and the death of Jesus (Ig. Tr. 9.1; Ig. Smyr. 1.2) before the eyes of the heavenly, terrestrial and subterranean powers (Ig. Tr. 9.1 connected with the crucifixion, not with the ascension), his resurrection on which the believer's resurrection depends (Ig. Tr. 9.2; cf. Pol. Phil. 2.1 f. and I Clem. 24.1 ff., where however the resurrection is already regarded as parallel to the reawakening of nature). Jesus' exaltation to be the Ruler and Judge at God's right hand is emphasized (Pol. Phil. 2.1). Barn. contains no long comprehensive credal forms. In the Didache the prayers for the Lord's Supper could be mentioned, which extol Jesus the Servant of God as the One who reveals the Church, knowledge and immortality. In I Clem. only 36.1 f. is to be mentioned, where Christ is praised as the source of immortal knowledge and vision of God and the great prayer of the Church in 59 f. which calls on God 'through Jesus Christ thy beloved Servant.' It should certainly be remembered that conventional summaries are not yet official ecclesiastical formulas (J. W. D. Kelly, *Early Christian Creeds*, London, 1950, p. 13) and that hymns are not creeds in the strict sense of the word (H. Conzelmann, *Schweiz. theol. Umschau*, 1955, p. 61 ff.). But we have restricted ourselves to those formulas which are clearly distinguished from their context, and moreover hymns in the NT have also an unmistakably credal character.

of the NT.[1] The significance of this statement should not be overlooked. Jesus Christ is the sole content of the Christian message. This is true in the most stringent sense. That means that it is not as if, in the last resort, it is not he himself who was meant but something else that he has brought, e.g. a new morality or even the forgiveness of sins. This may occasionally appear on the fringe[2] but then it is a more specific definition of Jesus Christ and has no independent value.

We must carefully safeguard this assertion. It is certainly true that credal formulas of this kind are quoted in connexion with a summons to ethical action or with a soteriological argument. It is therefore the opinion of the NT authors that they represent the answer to ethical and soteriological questions. But he, Jesus Christ himself, is this answer, not his ethics or his way of salvation which one could adopt quite apart from him, as if he were merely the bringer of this doctrine, the founder of this way of salvation. To the primitive Church Christology is the centre of her message. Of course it is, because the Church believes that this is the foundation of her salvation and her new life. But it is characteristic that there are hardly any comprehensive credal statements to be found which present the salvation granted or the form of the new life and from there point back to Jesus Christ as the cause.[3]

A second point must be clearly stated. In the majority of the formulas Jesus appears not only as the content of the confession but also formally as the subject of the proposition. At the same time however it must be maintained that he is often the subject

[1]Exceptions are the short statements in the Pastoral Epistles which confess God and Christ side by side (I Tim. 6.13; II Tim. 4.1); however the Pastoral Epistles have a tendency to place God in the centre rather than Christ. I Thess. 1.9 f. could be another exception but here the first part has probably been freely formulated by Paul.

[2]Tit. 2.12, 14; Acts 5.31; 10.43; 13.38.

[3]One can refer to Eph. 5.14. The call to repentance often appears in a stereotyped form. But one will also have to assume that ethical sayings of Jesus were handed down and collected at a very early date (G. Kittel, *ZNW* 43, 1950–1, p. 83 ff.; H. J. Holtzmann, *Lehrbuch der neutestamentlichen Theologie*, II, Tübingen, 1911, p. 232 f.) but they have obviously been used for the many concrete problems within the Church. They do not form the content of the *kerygma* to the world but the *didache* (C. H. Dodd, *The Apostolic Preaching and its Development*, London, 1944, p. 7 ff.). That which was really and fundamentally new to the Church was not found in them.

of a verb in the passive voice,[1] so that the formulas which present God as the subject and Jesus as the object of his work have substantially the same significance.[2] As far as the substance is concerned Jesus in the oldest statements appears as the subject only in connexion with his death,[3] which however was in fact a suffering and not, properly speaking, an active deed. Not until later does this suffering appear definitely as a conscious deed,[4] and it was probably even longer before the raising of Jesus became the resurrection, an act of Jesus himself.[5] Therefore the intention cannot have been to make metaphysical statements on Jesus which put him in God's place. In this sense one might rather say that Jesus withdraws before God. The reference is to God's *acting* on and in Jesus.

But it is true that no work of God other than that in Jesus is spoken of. Just for once the oneness of God may be preached in gentile territory.[6] And it cannot be denied that the oneness and also the creative work of God is described in formal expressions usually associated with OT, occasionally also with Stoic phrases. But the interesting and essential point is that in the NT all this amounts to no more than faint reminiscences. For one thing, whatever is said on this point never occurs independently of statements concerning Christ but as a more accurate definition of him who has acted in Christ;[7] and even then it appears in formal phrases at most and never in confessions or hymns proper.[8]

There is yet a third point to be stated which in part is already present in what we have just said. These credal forms almost

[1] I Cor. 15.4 (11.23 παρεδίδοτο); Rom. 1.3 f.; I Tim. 3.16; II Tim. 2.8; I Peter 3.18.

[2] Phil. 2.9; Col. 1.19; Acts 2.24, 32; 3.15; 4.10; 5.30 f.; 10.40; 13.30, 33 f.

[3] I Cor. 15.3; I Peter 3.18a (or ἔπαθεν).

[4] Phil. 2.6 ff.

[5] Cf. ἀναστῆναι Acts 10.41 (beside ἤγειρεν v. 40); also ch. 17.3; I Thess. 4.14; Mark 8.31; 9.9; Luke 24.7, 46; John 20.9). Besides the pouring out of the Spirit and the missionary commandment (Acts 2.33; 10.42) are described as acts of the risen Christ.

[6] I Thess. 1.9; cf. I Cor. 8.4–6; Acts 14.15–17; 17.22–31.

[7] I Cor. 8.6 is typical. The Stoic example and the context require only the confession to the εἷς θεός. This is modified into a confession of εἷς θεός καὶ εἷς κύριος.

[8] Cf. Kelly, *Early Christian Creeds*, pp. 19–23.

without any exception speak of *events*.[1] To the first Church Jesus Christ was not an idea but a sum of events. One should however not regard these events as 'historical' without qualification; indeed one might in a sense say that the 'historical aspect' of the appearance of Christ is very largely absent. His miracles, his preaching, his relation to the Baptist and similar matters are hardly ever mentioned. What are most frequently mentioned are those things which cannot at all events be confirmed by historical means: e.g. his exaltation to God's right hand, or even the resurrection, or the pre-existent Christ's decision to humble himself. And if historic events in the proper sense of the word are mentioned, then they are precisely not interesting as such but only in virtue of their interpretation, which is not open to purely historical examination. His death is important not simply as *brutum factum*, but as a gateway to glory or as a propitiation for sins. That is to say, these statements are always statements of faith. But this only means that the interpretation of those events is not open to everybody. It naturally does not alter their character as events.[2]

Jesus therefore is certainly not something like a symbol, merely revealing, representing and demonstrating a truth valid at all places and all times. Indeed one should express this even more sharply. It is not as if in the events here described something had come to light which also held good apart from these events, e.g. the fact that God is a gracious and not a wrathful God. Indeed, it is not even suggested that these events are important only because they are the historic cause of a condition which continues in the present, in the sense in which the Oath of Rütli and the wars of independence of the Swiss Confederacy are the foundations of Swiss democracy. Once again we must make it clear that the condition created by these events, e.g. the forgiveness of sin and the new life, hardly ever appear in the credal forms we have examined. This emphasizes the fact that every believer must enter into a direct relationship with Jesus Christ and the events reported about him. It would be possible to be a good Swiss citizen without any knowledge of the historic foundations

---

[1] This is rightly emphasized by E. F. Scott, *The Varieties of N.T. Religion*, 1946, pp. 18, 22, even though it is not sufficient to regard Jesus' 'personality' as the driving force behind the further development (p. 12 f.).

[2] Cf. J. M. Robinson, *Geschichtsverständnis*; *The Problem of History in Mark*.

of the state, and even if one regarded them as mere myths. But one cannot be a believer, in the sense of the NT, by accepting only the 'end product', the forgiveness of sin, or the new life, without Jesus Christ and what is reported of him. In this connexion the anchoring of this event in history is by no means irrelevant, even though historical data in the narrower sense of the word are lacking. For it cannot be doubted, and it is affirmed by all the credal forms, that even those events which are not accessible to historical investigation are indissolubly tied to the historical Jesus of Nazareth.[1]

[1]Col. 1.15–20 shows a further development. For the first stanza asserts that all things have their being 'in Christ' in virtue of their very creation; but in the course of the hymn this is corrected by a reference to the cross and the resurrection. The short expression 'Jesus is Lord' is not a credal form, properly speaking. But here too the name Jesus implies to the Church his life and death on earth and the title 'Lord' his exaltation.

XI

VARIATIONS IN THE CONFESSION OF CHRIST

(Survey of the Whole Development)

If now we inquire into the differences in the development, then this does not at all cancel out what has been said so far. The unity of the confession of Jesus remains the presupposition. The starting point of all confession is Jesus himself, his earthly life which ended in an humiliating death and his resurrection which the Church understood as his exaltation to God. The Church which confesses and proclaims these two things is, in the first instance, the community of those whom Jesus has called to follow him and whom he has taken with him on his way. That is how they came to share in it.

The homogeneity of the way of a disciple with the way of Jesus was at first visualized in an entirely realistic sense. It was something that took place on the roads of Palestine. It was a real *road* which brought fresh questions and answers, troubles and pleasures every day and every night. It was a being together *with* one another because the disciples shared every turn of Jesus' way. And the goal for which they were heading was their sharing in the *Kingdom of God*, the deliverance from the old world and entering into the new world. In all this it was never overlooked that the disciples' way and the way of Jesus were qualitatively distinguished. They had merely been taken up into his obedience and his promise. Admittedly such obedience has the promise of glory; but only in such a sense that here there could never again be any question of counting merit or reward. Such expectation is granted only to their staying with their Lord, to their faithfulness.

This actual staying with him ceased at Easter. After that the Church was forced to reflect on the theological question, how discipleship would continue henceforth.

The shallow rationalist interpretation that the way of Jesus is simply the example to be imitated has never had any decisive influence on the Church's preaching. It never, for example, occurred to anyone in the earliest Church to imitate Jesus' unmarried state in order to become his disciple in the full sense of the word. The first thing that the Church realized is this: if Jesus has gone the way in which Israel, in which the righteous in Israel have always been led, then he has done this in a final, fulfilling way. That is to say, the way of Israel has reached its goal, its eschatological consummation in him. In this sense words from the OT which referred to the way of Israel have been applied to Jesus. What God had planned for Israel had been fulfilled in him. The eschatological Israel was present in him. This perception has been retained by John and Paul when they speak of the vine and the branches or the body and the members, even though these words have been influenced by other thoughts as well. But it is also contained in those statements where Jesus identifies himself with his disciples: Acts 9.4 f.; 22.7 f.; 26.14 f.; Matt. 25.35–45; but also Mark 2.23 f. and similar passages.

If Jesus' way was now to be preached then there is no doubt that his death in humiliation and his exaltation to glory were in the first instance the decisive points. One could put the emphasis on his passion and death. In that case it was soon interpreted by the categories of vicarious suffering, propitiation and sacrifice. The pre-eminence of this way, its being 'for us', was thus stated in unmistakable terms. But it was also possible to put the main emphasis on his exaltation. And this gave rise to a copious history which we have examined in detail.

The lordship of the Exalted One was in the first place a continuation of the relationship which the earthly Jesus had had with his disciples. *He* took them with himself. *He* determined the way they were to go. And for the disciples of the earthly Jesus, as well as for the Church after Easter, this was a way leading into insecurity and distress, rejection and suffering. But, then as well as now, this way had the promise of exaltation to God's glory. For they shared the way with him who was the guarantee of the coming Kingdom of God. That is why from the outset this way had great hope and great consolation.

On the first line, which stressed the death of Jesus, it was

99

unmistakably asserted that the believer lives solely by what Jesus had done on this way through suffering to exaltation. Here too it is maintained equally unmistakably, that only he who allows himself to be taken by Jesus on this way with him, really understands and can confess what has happened there for him. The 'for us' holds good only in the 'with him'. But ultimately the two cannot be separated. For 'with him' is something that man simply cannot achieve by himself. This is already grace, a gift. From the very beginning it is a being taken with him. In the further development of the Church's preaching this is underlined with increasing clarity also on this second line.

Firstly, the message of Jesus' lordship acquires increasing importance. At the outset this also implies the truth that the disciple who has been allowed to become obedient to this Lord is also sure of being guarded and supported. If Jesus is the Lord of his Church then he is also Lord over those who persecute her. Ps. 110, which became important at a very early date, announces the subjection of all enemies, and the same thing is said in Ps. 2. Therefore Heb. 10.12 f., on the basis of Ps. 110, looks for the subjection of all enemies to him who is at the right hand of God. And the same idea appears in I Cor. 15.34. Here the expectation is still entirely derived from Judaism, because the ultimate victory is expected only at the *parousia*, like the expectation in Jewish Apocalyptic (cf. also Matt. 25.41; Rev. 19.20; 20.14). There, actual hostile nations and their rulers had long been identified with demoniacal powers and forces. Therefore one need not wonder that Phil. 2.10 f. again expresses this subjection of all in a quotation from the OT, but at the same time defines 'all' more precisely as 'those in heaven, on earth and under the earth'.[1] But while in this passage one must still doubt whether this is regarded as an accomplished fact or not, in I Peter 3.22 this subjection is proclaimed as having taken place at the ascension. This is not just something new either. The casting out of demons by Jesus had already represented this victory over all powers.

In this manner the assertion of the lordship of Jesus has been extended. Increasingly it assumed the aspect of protection and safekeeping. We therefore need not wonder that on this line it is emphasized above all that Jesus 'hath overcome the world', so

[1] The '*things*' of EVV. are not in the Greek.

that a disciple need no longer be afraid ('Be of good cheer', John 16.33), or that he has delivered his people from the bondage of the fear of death (Heb. 2.14 f.). Here, not the promise of deliverance from sin but of deliverance from fear is placed in the centre. But it could be that this very fear is nothing other than the sin of man emancipated from God.

Closely connected with this is the fact that the idea of the disciples' following Jesus is also expanded. From the beginning his discipleship was not confined to the part of the way within this earthly aeon. When the Son of man will sit in his throne then his twelve disciples will be on the throne together with him (Luke 22.30). They will be sitting near him, perhaps directly at his right and his left hand (Mark 10.40). Certainly, this also will be a mere gift and there can be no question of any guarantee. However much this may be promised to the faithfulness of the disciple who remains with Jesus to the end, yet it cannot be gained by merit. The Father alone will arrange this; Jesus is not able to distribute reserved tickets. But in the hope of such communion in the coming Kingdom the disciples now already share the earthly way of Jesus. This is a moving 'out of the old world'. The more emphatic the thought of protection and safekeeping by the Lord, the more emphatic also the character of this discipleship as a gift proves to be, the more also is the following of the disciple regarded as a following 'on the way to heaven', to the glory of the Father.

But in yet a third point a definite development shows itself. The thought of Jesus' humiliation also receives an extraordinary expansion. Independent of whether the words 'I have come . . .' are his or not, Jesus' consciousness of his mission already contains the claim that in his words and deeds God himself comes to man. This was true at the outset for everyone who let himself be called to follow him. As soon as the Church after Easter preached him she proclaimed that he was the One in whom God's final, conclusive act had taken place, the One in whom God's whole will of grace had been fulfilled. To the Jews of those days all that God had decided for the salvation of his people had long been present 'in heaven' before it takes place upon earth. Thus the tabernacle and the Law are pre-existent but also the whole history of God's saving acts. Above all the Messiah also is pre-existent with God.[1] The OT and late Jewish statements on the wisdom of God have had a great influence on the rise of assertions concerning the pre-existence of Jesus.[2] This is shown by the texts. The earliest text, I Cor. 8.6, depicts Jesus as the Mediator of creation, like the Wisdom in the OT. I Cor. 10.4 applies words spoken about the Wisdom to Jesus.[3] The quotation of Rom. 10.6 is applied to Wisdom in I Baruch 3.29 f. and the wording of Gal. 4.4 is influenced by Wisd. 9.10, 17, where Wisdom and the Holy Spirit of God are sent from heaven.[4] Even if John 1.1 ff. cannot be interpreted in the light of the Wisdom literature alone, yet the assertion that the Logos was with God and that he came into the world have their origin there. Phil. 2.6–8 certainly goes further than the Wisdom idea, but it adopts the typically Jewish motive of the self-humiliation of the suffering righteous one and not that of the Gnostic saviour myth. The absolute pre-eminence of the way of Jesus has thus been stated in an unmistakable manner. In him the hearer of the message does not meet just an itinerant philosophical preacher or a mere ethical example. In him God himself meets us. This statement here has the same function as the words 'for us' in the plan of vicarious suffering. 'For your sakes he became poor' (II Cor. 8.9) substantially corresponds with

[1]Preliminary stages of this conception are phrases like Isa. 49.16 or Ezek. 40–48 where quite realistically the prophet has to wade now through the future temple brook (ch. 47.3–5). For the pre-existence of the tabernacle and the law cf. *Str-B.* III, p. 700 ff.; Jub. 3.10 f.; 4.5, 32; Test.A. 7.5; for the history of salvation engraved in heavenly tablets: Jub. 23.32; 31.32; 32.28; TestL. 5.3 f.; Test.A. 2.10. The pre-existence of the Son of man is found Eth.En. 39.6; 40.5; 48.3. Yet it can be said on the whole that the pre-existence of the Messiah is no problem to Judaism but that the earthly life of Jesus of Nazareth is (W. L. Knox, Harvard Th.R. 1946, p. 231, note 3).

[2]Already in the OT it is often said that God comes down to intervene in human history. In a later period this is said of his Word or his Spirit. Eventually these appear personified in the form of God's Wisdom, a parallel figure to God's Logos (Wisd. 9.16). This is pre-existent (Prov. 8.30 f.; Ecclus. 1.4; 24.9) with God (Prov. 8.30; Ecclus. 1.1), is seated with him in his throne (Wisd. 9.4; 8.3) and co-operates in the creation (Wisd. 9. 2, 9; Prov. 3.19; 8.27). She moves through heaven, chaos and world before she settles in Israel (Ecclus. 24.5 ff.). As God's messenger she calls the world back to God (Prov. 8.1 ff., 17 ff., 35 f.; 9.5 f.; Ecclus. 24.17–22) and disillusioned returns to the angels (Eth.En. 42.1 f.). All this furnished the language and the conceptions by which the Church could speak of the advent of Jesus. Cf. also the descent of the *shekhina* from the seventh heaven to the tabernacle of the Covenant, H. Traub, *Th.Wb.* V, pp. 511, 527 f.

[3]Philo, *Leg. All.* 2.86; *Quod deterius* 115.

[4]Cf. E. Schweizer in *EvTh*, 1959, p. 65 ff.

'my body for you' (I Cor. 11.24). It would also have been possible for the Church to have recourse to the individual's experience of conversion, in order to retain what was contained in Jesus' calling the fishermen by the Lake of Galilee or Levi in the house of toll. But rightly this answer has not been given because it would not have expressed the pre-eminence of the work of Jesus and the character of this event as grace with sufficient clarity. Here man's religion could easily have been substituted for God's work. But the Church insisted that everything depends on the fact that *he* who was equal to God humbled himself in order to call us and to take us with him on *his* way.

In detail this can assume very different forms. The conception of the Epistle to the Hebrews is the most simple. Only in such humiliation does Jesus become the High Priest who can really understand men. Here the thought of being understood, of being taken to him has become predominant. But the statement can also be turned to the effect that Jesus shows the way of passion to be full of meaning by taking the way of humility, by being exalted and glorified precisely in his taking of the way of obedience, in suffering and humiliation, as is the case in the Gospel according to St John. He who himself experiences glorification in the midst of suffering takes his disciples with him on this way which bestows the glory of oneness with the Father already in the midst of suffering. Not only *after* obedient suffering, but in the midst of it, is found the exaltation to the Father, is one taken out of the reality of the old world. Thus this way means to a disciple an 'exercise' in faith, in which a disciple experiences his sharing in the glory of God. Only so can he also be a credible witness of his Lord, in that he is permitted while he himself goes this way, in his turn to take brothers with him. Similarly in Heb. 12.2 the Lord who has gone before is certainly an example, which one looks up to, but is at the same time the 'pioneer and perfecter of faith'. Similarly in John 13.15 his humble service on the last night is certainly both an example to his disciples but at the same time far more than this (John 13. 8b, 10). And similarly the hymn Phil. 2.6–11 has been placed by Paul in the context of v.5 with its remarkable statement. Jesus' way may be an example; but at the same time it is far more: what is already true for them 'in Jesus', they must now also realize in their thinking and in their dealing with one another.

XII

THE 'TRANSLATION' OF THE MESSAGE
FOR THE HELLENISTIC CHURCH

THIS development of the preaching of the message became particularly important when it reached the Hellenistic world.[1] Hellenistic man is no longer the man of the classical period. At one time Plato and Aristotle appealed to men to watch the starry sky. To the people of their days the eternally unchanging course of the heavenly bodies represented the harmony of the cosmos. This course of the stars embodied the eternal laws of God which determine the whole universe. God and the world were experienced as a unity. But the world had changed in the centuries which separate Hellenism from Greece's classical period. The time when the Greek *polis* could guard its freedom with a number of courageous and wise men was irrevocably past. Alexander the Great with his gigantic armies of mercenaries had marched through half the world. New arms had been invented against which the courage of the individual could do nothing. The small city-states of Greece had been condemned to impotence. And what good does it do the Stoic if with a certain impressive pathos he declares that the whole world is his *polis*? For this pretentious phrase is in fact a retreat from active political life and an admission that he can no longer exercise any practical influence on this '*polis*'. Thus the eternally unchanging course of the heavenly bodies becomes more and more the expression of a feeling of being at the mercy of a terrible fate. *Heimarmene*, blind fate is the highest god.[2] All things take their unalterable course. The heavens have become brazen, blind to the destiny of man, deaf to their cries. Unmoved the stars pursue their course and drag the whole universe with them in their orbit. Like the wheels of a machine turning mercilessly,

[1] Cf. p. 27, note 3.
[2] For parallels in the Isis cult cf. Apuleius, *Metamorph*. XI, 25 (also VI.15) and *Corpus Inscr. Lat*. XIV, 2867 (*Isityche*).

without taking any notice of whom they crush, so fate takes its course. The heavenly, divine world is beyond this cosmos. At one time Greek man was at home in this world; now he has become a stranger. All his longings and desires centre in the attempt to escape from this world and its merciless fate and to partake of that heavenly, divine world. Thus magic and superstition have the upper hand. Dream-books and astrological works play an important part. By all possible formulas and practices man of the Hellenistic time endeavours to overcome the *heimarmene* and to escape from its hold.

If Jesus is preached to this man as the Lord, then this must mean to him that Jesus is Lord also over fate, over the evil powers and forces which so far have kept his life in bondage. To begin with this is perfectly right. Every genuine confession answers *those* questions which are really asked. And the decisive question of the Hellenist is the question concerning the meaning of his life in general, concerning the fate to which his life and his world are subject. Thus he accepts particularly eagerly what was *a priori* implied in Jesus' being the Lord: namely that Jesus is Lord also over all powers and forces, over the demons as well as over hostile persecutors. Thereby this aspect acquires a new and unexpected importance. Jesus here assumes the place of the *heimarmene*. As the Exalted One he becomes the One who holds fate, the whole course of the world, in his hands, because no power of fate can match him.

But there is more. We already said that the longing of Hellenism was towards finding ways and means to escape from this world and to reach that higher, heavenly world which is above all the spheres, in which the powers and forces reign. In ecstasy he already experiences such deliverance of his soul, and for the time after his death he expects that his soul will ascend to that divine world from which it came down at birth. He now hears the message of him who has already ascended to the Father and who desires to take his people with him on this way to glory. To him therefore the message of following Jesus means in the first place the fulfilment of this longing of his for an ascension into the 'higher' world. This too is still right. The Hellenist thereby adopts something that was always implied in the hope of the Church. The only thing is that the spatial pattern which no longer sees the goal of its longing in the future but in the higher, heavenly world, has become the decisive one.

Finally, if Jesus is really preached to the man of this time as the One in whom salvation is present, in whom God himself meets the believer, then this means for him that in Jesus God's higher world has broken into this earthly world. In his mode of conception he cannot express this in any other way than by speaking of the One who descended from God's world into his world. This also is still a correct reproduction of the original testimony. What the first Church said when she confessed Jesus as the eschatological Fulfiller of all the prophecies, this the Hellenistic Church says by confessing him as the One who came from heaven. She thereby guards against the obvious misunderstanding that she had to proclaim only an itinerant philosopher-preacher or a 'divine man', as Hellenism knew them in multitude. The Hellenistic Church has thus raised in its fundamental sense the universally valid statement, and expresses in her own language what already held good for Levi when God himself approached him by the calling of Jesus and grace happened.

And yet all this could be altogether wrong. There is a great danger in thinking of the overcoming of powers and forces in a purely physical sense. According to this conception he who ascended to heaven would have overcome physically all the demoniacal figures which occupy the strongholds in the spiritual spheres between earth and heaven and thus bar to men the access to God's world.[1] The discipleship of the Church would then have to be understood in an equally physical sense. By the sacrament the believer would then be united with the heavenly Saviour, taken up into the physically conceived heavenly body and thus deified. Though the earthly body might be dissolved in death, the divine substance would remain and, delivered from all material fetters, would be drawn upward into the heavenly body where it already belongs according to its true nature. In the last resort the incarnation would be no more than an epiphany. The form of humiliation could then be nothing more than make believe before the demons. Indeed, one could go even further: for the whole message of the descent of the Saviour could then be a mere myth, a presentation

[1] Cf. Asc. Is. 11.23 ff., where the worship of all the demons shows their defeat.

interpreted purely symbolically of what always happens to the human soul when it falls from the divine homeland into earthly matter. This argument would have landed us in the Gnosticism of the second century.[1]

[1]Documentary evidence of the Gnostic myth: E. Schweizer, article πνεῦμα, *Th.Wb.* VI, p. 391 f.; for the Hellenistic myth of the soul and the belief in destiny cf. *Erniedrigung und Erhöhung*, par. 15.

XIII

THE PRESERVATION OF THE ORIGINAL MESSAGE IN THE 'TRANSLATION'

WHAT W. Bauer has demonstrated in respect of the history of dogma during the first centuries[1] also holds good to a certain extent for the history of dogma within the NT: heresy stands at the beginning of new insight. The witnesses of the NT, above all Paul, encountered the enthusiastic interpretation of the Hellenistic Church and had to formulate their theological statements while listening to that Church and her questions and warding off her mistaken formulations. This is how those statements acquired their sharp contours and many old views received a quite new significance. The dangers just mentioned have certainly not been present to the same extent everywhere and have not everywhere been equally energetically averted. But in all the passages we have discussed the questions of the Hellenistic world seem to have challenged, and therefore also had a part in shaping, the proclamation of the message. But the message has not succumbed to it.

In the NT the lordship of Jesus in the first place is his lordship of his Church. Only where this is acknowledged does the assertion of his lordship over the powers hold good as well. That is why in the credal statements the declaration about the subjugation of the powers and forces, which has already taken place, is accepted with so much hesitation. It appears for certain first in I Peter 3.22. But even in hymns like Phil. 2.6–11 and I Tim. 3.16, where the assertion of Jesus' lordship over the powers takes a central place, the actual goal is the *Church*'s adoration of her Lord. In the second case this is underlined by emphasizing that this lordship of Jesus takes effect in the mission in which the confessing Church is actively engaged. But also in the Fourth Gospel

[1]*Rechtgläubigkeit und Ketzerei im ältesten Christentum*, Tübingen, 1934.

and the Epistle to the Hebrews Jesus' commandments to his Church receive remarkably strong emphasis and are the real concern of the texts. That is why in John 12.31 the casting out of the prince of this world does not come about as the result of his being overcome physically by the Lord at his ascension, but at the moment when Jesus practises the ultimate obedience, accepts the way of the cross, and thus achieves full union with the Father. Therefore this defeat of Satan is not simply true for all the people. For the people are standing by without understanding and only think that they have heard a thunder-clap or at best some angelic being. This final defeat of the prince of this world is true and real only for those who hear Jesus' word and share in his obedience.

The demarcation of the message against the danger of rising Gnosticism, and the systematic connexion of the statements about the exaltation of Jesus and those about his atoning death, are to be found most strongly emphasized in the writings of Paul. For Paul too can speak of the overcoming of all powers and forces. This cannot be too strongly emphasized. How could he then be afraid of those Hellenistic formulations with their exaggerated enthusiasm?[1] It depends entirely on how they are interpreted. What then does Paul really proclaim when he speaks of the exalted Lord's triumph over all the demons?

To Paul the powers finally dispatched by Jesus are: Law, Sin, Death. *They* are the demoniacal powers over which Jesus' victory is to be proclaimed. This becomes most clear in Gal. 4.3, 8–10. The enslavement of man under the powers of this world before the coming of Jesus consisted in his being a slave of the law. A return to legalism, similar to that which threatened to take place in Galatia, is therefore a revival of the already defeated powers. By his having been set free from the *Law* man has been delivered from his enslavement to the powers. Whether as a pious Jew he wished to give meaning to his life by a hunt for a righteousness of his own through scrupulous observance of the law, or whether as a pagan he desired to do the same by amassing wealth or by living a sensual life, ultimately amounts to the same thing. Man has been delivered by Jesus from this search for the

[1]Yet (contrary to W. Schmithals, *Die Gnosis in Korinth*, 1956), I do not think that this was a Gnostic saviour myth (cf. p. 125 ff.).

preservation of his life by his own strength. Only thus is he free from the powers. So in Paul's writings the assertion of Jesus' lordship over all the powers is unmistakably connected with the message of his death on the cross which has brought men justification. Therefore Paul does not formulate in physical terms: 'the powers are dead'; on the contrary he proclaims to the Church that they are dead 'to us', that because of Jesus' sacrifice they can no longer do anything 'to us' (I Cor. 8.6; Rom. 8.38 f.).

The same must be said in connexion with the second point. In the Church of Jesus discipleship has always implied in the first place the obedience of the believer in his daily conduct. Only where it is thus understood, is it also the promise of participation in Jesus' exaltation to glory. No sacramental communion can take the place of *this* fellowship. In the hymns Phil. 2.6–11 and I Tim. 3.16 this is kept in mind, in that the Church confesses itself to be the Church of the Exalted One precisely by the singing of these phrases. This is emphasized even more strongly by the fact that in the NT they occur only in a context which explicitly calls for an actualizing of this faith in ethical steadfastness. Again the Gospel according to John and the Epistle to the Hebrews leave no doubt on this point. Looking up to him who went the way to suffering and shame the Church stretches her tired legs and unflinchingly continues her own way to suffering (Heb. 12.1–13). And the connexion of the branches with the vine is not simply a fact of nature but proceeds from the fact that they, the branches, can do nothing without him, the vine. But for that very reason they are to keep his commandments and go the way which he himself has gone before them (John 15.1–21). The paradox formulation of the Fourth Gospel, that the exaltation and glorification take place precisely *in* the lowliness of obedience, is perhaps the sharpest demarcation in the NT from the idea of an escape into a better beyond. It is *in the midst of* the world that freedom from the world becomes a reality in obedient, confident fulfilling of the commandments. Thus the disciple has been given courage for his daily task.

This again receives its sharpest outline in the writings of Paul. Here too one can say that Paul is not afraid to borrow Hellenistic expressions. He does this to such an extent that A. Schweitzer thought that Paul had to be interpreted entirely from this point of view.[1] It is certainly possible that Paul conceived of the body of Christ in a material manner, as a kind of fluid issuing from the Exalted One and embracing all those who belong to him. After all, the Hellenist can conceive of power only in the form of substance.[2] And again: one cannot express the alliance of the Church with her Lord too realistically. Yet his realistic expressions are merely the material which Paul uses to express this reality. But we must ask again what actually he means by them.

When Paul speaks of the body of Christ this does in fact mean that there is a sphere in which the blessing of what happened on the cross continues to act, and in which he who through his resurrection was exalted to be the Lord exercises this his lordly dominion; namely the Church. To be taken up into the body of Christ is in fact a very real event. It means: to come within the 'power-field' which is determined by the crucifixion and resurrection of Jesus, that is to say, to come under his blessing and his dominion. That is why Paul by the 'body of Christ' into which we are taken up, can also mean the body that was sacrificed on the cross (I Cor. 10.16, cf. 17; 11.24, 27, 29; Rom. 7.4; cf. Eph. 2.16). For the believers have been taken up into this body of Christ because if 'one died for all, therefore all died' (II Cor. 5.14).[3] In the body of Christ crucified on the cross we have already been crucified together with him. For Jesus has died there as the Representative of Israel, who in his obedient dying included all those who were to belong to him.[4] But for this very reason, this belonging to him, this inclusion in his body can only come about each time by a fresh act of faith in what happened there. In Paul's Epistles this is shown particularly clearly by the fact that he avoids the assertion that the Church has risen with Christ. Through baptism she was crucified and buried with him, but being raised with him is something that takes place in the conduct of the believer until his final resurrection at the last day (Rom. 6.4 f.). Not

---

[1] *Die Mystik des Apostels Paulus*, Tübingen, 1930, Engl. tr. *The Mysticism of Paul the Apostle* by W. Montgomery, London, 1931; cf. also certain statements in J. A. T. Robinson, *The Body*, London, 1952, who however argues more guardedly and is rightly interested in Paul's realism.

[2] Evidence in *Th.Wb.*, article πνεῦμα, VI, p. 390, note 347.

[3] Cf. L. S. Thornton, *The Common Life in the Body of Christ*, p. 46, 298; also W. Hahn, *Gottesdienst und Opfer Christi*, 1951, pp. 51, 73.

[4] Cf. p. 119 ff.

until the Epistle to the Colossians is this spoken of as something that has already taken place, but even there it is covered by the necessary qualification. For firstly it comes about 'through faith', while being buried with Christ took place 'in baptism'; and secondly this new life is at all events a hidden life of which, it is true, one can speak in the indicative, but to which at the same time one has to summon in the imperative (Col. 2.12; 3.1–4).[1]

In the old words on discipleship the bond of the disciples with their Lord consisted in their daily sharing his way. We have found that the same is true of the time of the Church after Easter in the Synoptic Gospels and John. It is no different with Paul. At times formulations borrowed from the mystery religions may have influenced his 'Christ-mysticism', as far as the wording is concerned; but the great difference is the fact that what is the only centre there is *not* stated at all here, namely, that man has already been raised to new life by the saviour-god, that he has already been deified. If the Corinthians did not believe in the resurrection at the second advent, then this was because they had adopted the interpretation of the Hellenistic religions. In agreement with Hymenaeus and Philetus (II Tim. 2.18) they thought that the resurrection had already taken place, that the apotheosis had already taken effect under the outward veil of the body, and that the incorruptible, physical bodily existence of the new man had already come, so that death would be no more than the falling away of the earthly body. It was to meet them that Paul has to make the assertion, completely impossible for all the mystery religions, that his sharing in Christ is to be found in his suffering of persecution.[2] The body of Christ, as the sphere of blessing, in which that which happened on the cross continues to act, is at the same time the territory of Christ's dominion, in which the exalted Lord claims the service of his disciples every day.

Finally the proclamation on the third point is quite plain. Everywhere in the NT it is maintained that Christ really did become man, indeed that he became flesh. This thought is entirely foreign to a Hellenist. The most he knows is of ephemeral

---

[1] Cf. N. Clark, *An Approach to the Theology of the Sacraments*, London, 1956, pp. 81–83.
[2] Cf. p. 48, 91.

epiphanies of the gods.[1] This is true also of the Fourth Gospel and the Epistle to the Hebrews. Even if the term 'flesh' in John 1.14 does not include all that is meant by the Pauline term,[2] it comprises at least the full obedience of the Son in this earthly sphere. That is why this Gospel often underlines all kinds of concrete details even more than the Synoptic Gospels. The Epistle to the Hebrews goes so far as to mention not only cries and tears but even to state that Jesus learnt obedience (Heb. 5.6). And in the passage where the incarnation of the pre-existent Christ appears for the first time in our tradition, it is explicitly understood as an act of obedience and self-humiliation (Phil. 2.6 f.), that is to say entirely parallel to the meaning which his road to humiliation and shame in the crucifixion already had for the earliest Church. But also in I Tim. 3.16 the unmistakable expression 'flesh' is used to indicate the sphere in which the epiphany of the Son of man took place.

Again Paul has maintained this clearly. Here too Paul shows no fear of Hellenistic terminology. He who lived in that higher world in a form equal to God has in fact come down to man. How could that which his advent means ever be stated sufficiently realistically? But again there is no doubt that this is a real incarnation, that he really did become man, and that this advent means self-humiliation and obedience, as in the old conception of the suffering Righteous One. 'For your sakes he became *poor*' (II Cor. 8.9). And when Paul in Phil. 2.6–11 quotes a hymn of the Church it should be observed that this actually mentions the form of a servant in which Jesus met man. The specifically Pauline interpretation of this fact is shown in Gal. 4.4. Here the birth of Jesus is identical with his being placed under the law. But this obedient submission to the law reaches its climax where the law has its ultimate effect and causes Jesus' shameful execution: Gal. 2.19; 3.13; Rom. 8.3. Thus here too the incarnation and the crucifixion are closely connected.

[1] *Corp. Herm.* 10.25: 'None of the heavenly gods will leave heaven and come down to earth.' Details in *Erniedrigung und Erhöhung*, par. 15.
[2] Cf. the author's article σάρξ in *Th.Wb*.

XIV

CONCLUSION

A RICH development has certainly taken place. We have given a summary of it in ch. XI. One can schematically characterize its extreme points by saying that on the line which was of particular importance to the Hellenists, the line which we have followed, the creed contains the descent of the pre-existent Christ and the ascent to lordship of the Exalted One, while on the other line it contains the ascension in the resurrection from the dead and the descent in his second advent.[1] But even where no reference is made to the *parousia* but to the atoning death instead, the distinctions are clear. If, to conclude, we compare once more two statements in I Cor. 15.3–5 and Phil. 2.6–11, both in the writings of Paul, then this becomes obvious. In I Cor. 15.3 the humanity of Jesus is the natural starting point. The *fact* of his humanity and his death is no part of the creed. Only the interpretation of his death as having been suffered 'for our sins' makes it this. Entirely different is Phil. 2.6 f. Here his being equal to God is the obvious starting point. His humanity is already the effect of an act based on a decision of the pre-existent Christ. Moreover in I Cor. 15.4 the resurrection is the concluding statement. It is God's affirmative answer to the particular death of Jesus which has been manifested. Quite different again is Phil. 2.9–11, where the resurrection is not even mentioned, because the dominion of the Exalted One, to whom all powers in heaven, on the earth and under the earth are subjected, is the goal of the whole passage. Further I Cor. 15.3 f. maintains twice that everything has happened 'according to the Scriptures', that is to say, as the fulfilment of a history with an eschatological aim. On the other hand, in Phil. 2.6–11, the spatial concepts of above and below, of being *humbled* and being *exalted*, play the main parts. There is something more profound behind these observations: in I Cor. 15.3 it is explicitly said that these

---

[1] Thus explicitly in I Thess. 1.10. On the contrary the Exalted One's rise to dominion and his second advent do not appear closely connected.

events have happened 'for our sins', that is to say, for the benefit of the Church. This is lacking in Phil. 2.6–11. For here the Church, in singing the hymn, is present herself at this adoration of the all-embracing dominion of Jesus, which is the aim of the whole creed. That is why on this line we particularly find hymns, while on the other line doctrinal formulae appear. It is obvious: the questions which are answered in each case are not the same. I Cor. 15.3–5 was formed in a Church for which sins were the real problem. Her first question was: how can I ever be righteous before God? That is why the main emphasis here is on the death of Jesus. She remembers this death and is glad, comforted and confident because of it. Phil. 2.6–11 presupposes a Church for which the meaninglessness of life and the impossibility of eluding a blind fate is the greatest distress. For her the most important question is: how do I escape from the dominion of these powers? Here therefore the decisive emphasis is on the exaltation of Jesus. The Church surrenders to this by singing this hymn, and under this she lives, day by day. It is quite clear that there are dangers on both lines. Where the 'for us' was the sole centre there was also the possibility of misunderstanding a purely academic acceptance of truth. Where the 'with him' was the sole centre, over-enthusiastic anticipation was the danger.

Therefore the two assertions have been kept close together in the NT. For eventually they are one. For this comfortless fatalism of the Hellenists, their enslavement to the belief in a blind fate, this paralysing self-surrender is nothing other than the particular form in which apostasy from the living God, sin, appears in their case. And, conversely, this very praise of him who has humbled himself in obedience and has therefore become Lord over all the powers, is particularly necessary to a Palestinian. For this is an expression of the fact that a man not only intellectually believes that Christ died 'for our sins' and that by raising him God has said 'yes' to this; but that, day by day, as a believer, he *lives* in this liberty now granted to him. The NT knits the two assertions closely together. This has been done with ultimate theological power in the Gospel according to John, where the 'with him' is particularly underlined as the 'for us' is in Paul's Epistles. Here there cannot be Greek and Jew, Hellenist and Palestinian, but Christ is all and in all (cf. Col. 3.11).

Both assertions have come from the same source. The picture of Jesus who called the disciples to follow him and walked with them on the roads of Palestine has retained its force. It has guarded the Church against lapsing into a merely academic acceptance of a *doctrine* of atonement and into an enthusiastic Gnosis, thinking in purely physical terms. It has also saved her from a corruption of the message into an ethic determined by an example, or a morality exemplified in the figure of a teacher. It has determined her preaching through all the changing stages of development, and yet given her the liberty to make a real confession which answered burning questions, not those which no longer existed. Thus the exalted Lord accompanies his Church through decades and through centuries, as he accompanied his disciples when he walked on earth.

The same truth has been expressed in different patterns. It is impossible to 'distil' a 'pure' creed. Every generation must proclaim the gospel in its own terms. It is foolish to withhold belief from the creeds of another generation simply because we cannot use their language today. But it is just as foolish to assent to all the creeds together, as if orthodoxy were like some cafeteria where you are obliged to eat something of everything. The New Testament attempts neither a pure creed nor a collection of all possible creeds. To be sure, a purely 'Greek' formulation, without eschatology, would have reduced the gospel to mysticism; and a purely 'Hebrew' proclamation, without 'Greek' clarification, would have reduced Christianity to just another Jewish sect. Nevertheless, the New Testament contributors were courageous enough to be one-sided. They made their choice, and preached the message in terms their hearers could grasp, opposing clearly the special dangers of their particular time and place. The Palestinian church proclaimed the incomparable uniqueness and pre-eminence of Jesus Christ in terms of God's eschatological action, the Hellenistic church in terms of Christ's heavenly nature. Must our younger generation (or, to take a quite different example, the Japanese people) first be converted to a Hebrew or Greek way of thinking in order to be able to receive the gospel? Or may we, without denying the old creeds, proclaim the same truth in the West, perhaps in terms of the meaning of God's acts for our existence, and in Japan, perhaps in quite different terms?

APPENDICES

A. THE 'FIRST MAN'

One would have to write a monograph if one were to give a more or less comprehensive account of scholarly research on the subject. Some mere hints will have to suffice here.

Indian myth speaks of a deity of light which, overcome by darkness in the very beginning, died and thus gave rise to the formation of the world and of man but in his inner self remained intact, in order at a given time to continue the battle against darkness and to gain the victory.[1] While in India the idea is a reincarnation of the 'first man' at the beginning of each period, in *Iran* he appears as the eschatological warrior of light, who brings the ultimate victory at the end of time.[2] But the expectation of an eschatological saviour who is to bring back paradise comes late in Iran.[3] Only in the late Pahlavi texts is the 'first man' a heavenly being, who becomes a victim of the evil powers and from which the human race descends. Formerly the first man Gayomart is only put in the foreground and connected with the eschatological saviour Saoshyant by the formula 'from the man Gaya to the victorious Saoshyant'.[4] But the antiquity of the conception that Gayomart will rise again first, that he is the first rational high priest, the pioneer of all men in true life, and that he ascends to the archangel, remains doubtful.[5] In the *Semitic* world one finds the conception of the first patriarch who is depicted in royal glory. This is done above all in the remarkable passage Ezek. 28.12 ff. where the myth is already related to the king of Tyrus: 'Thou wast in Eden, the garden of God, full of wisdom and consummate beauty; every precious stone was thy covering . . .; in the day

[1]For general information cf. L. Troje, *R.G.G.*[2] V, p. 1416 f.
[2]S. Mowinckel, 'Urmensch und Königsideologie', *StTh*, II/1, 1949, p. 72.
[3]W. Staerk, *Soter* II, p. 247 f.; The 'cyclical' appearance of the First Man in Iran is discussed by G. Widengren, *ZRGG* IV, 1952, p. 113.
[4]Cf. W. Manson, *Jesus the Messiah*, London, 1943, pp. 179 ff.
[5]Cf. G. Quispel, *Eranos-Jahrbuch* 1953, p. 229 f.

that thou wast created I have placed thee on firm foundations(?); I appointed thee as a cherub; I put thee on the holy mountain of God; thou walkedst up and down in the midst of stones of fire; thou wast perfect in thy ways' (new tr.). This original father has probably no connexion with the first man of Iranian origin and has not been brought into relation with it until later, in later Judaism.[1]

Such *speculations on Adam* were wide spread in later Judaism, especially where this had a strongly Hellenistic character. The many graphic accounts of the original glory of Adam are undoubtedly pre-christian:[2] 'The glory of Adam is above all who have ever lived' (Ecclus. 49.16). '(Wisdom) gave him power to have dominion over all things' (Wisd. 10.2). He was formed in perfection, from pure original matter, as a 'divine scion like the elder Logos', the 'image of God', king, priest and prophet (Philo., quoted by Staerk, p. 65 f.). But similar statements also occur in probably pre-christian Palestinian literature. Adam is the second angel, ruler over the earth, unique, and he sees the higher world (*The Slavonic Book of Enoch* 30.8 ff.; 31.2; cf. 58.3 and IV Ezra 6.54), so that Satan cannot approach him who is like God at all but has to have recourse to Eve (31.6). The *Vita Adae* 12 ff. goes still further: all the angels have to worship Adam; Satan refuses to do this and is therefore thrown down[3] and must leave his vacated throne to Adam (47). Beside this the picture appears of Noah as a glorious man, miraculous, angel-like, whose eyes illuminate all things as the sun and who immediately after his birth stood up to praise God.[4] Philo depicts him as a second patriarch (*Vita Mosis* II.60; 65; *de Aoramo* 46; *Quaest. in Genesim* 1.96; 2.96). But the idea that Adam is passing through the world in ever new forms is absent from ancient biblical or extra-biblical sources of Judaism.[5] This does not appear until the pseudo-Clementine literature (Homilies 3.20), though Schoeps is probably wrong in assuming

[1] Mowinckel, *StTh.* II/1, p. 72 ff.; disputed by Gressmann and many others, also by A. Bentzen, *Messias—Moses redivivus—Menschensohn*, Zürich, 1948, p. 38 f. Cf. Mowinckel, *He that cometh*, p. 346 ff.

[2] Staerk, *Soter* II/1, p. 7 ff.; Quispel, *Eranos-Jahrbuch*, 1953, p. 215 ff.

[3] Bousset-Gressmann, *Religion des Judentums*, p. 352; parallels in Quispel, p. 226, note 57.

[4] Eth. Enoch 106.2 f.; these chapters on Noah cannot be dated with any certainty.

[5] Staerk, *Soter* II/1, p. 139 f.

that it is there derived only from the prophecy of the reappearing prophet, Deut. 18.15–18.[1] It could have been derived from a pre-christian doctrine of the seven prophets,[2] but even this would not yet be a doctrine of the incarnation of the first man. H. Odeberg, it is true, asks whether this doctrine is not already behind the speculations concerning Enoch,[3] but this cannot be proved. But the expectation that the Messiah will bring back paradise and be the eschatological king of paradise is pre-Christian.[4] It is difficult to say whether this is due to the influence of the Iranian, pre-Zoroastrian king of paradise, Yima, who is the first man and later on also the lord of the time of salvation (Yasna 9.4 ff.). Judaism and Parseeism have probably mutually influenced one another. In this way the idea that he loses his glory on account of his falsehood has later been assigned to Yima.[5]

With the necessary caution one can thus say: 'The concept of the first man as the ideal man, as well as the doctrine of the restitution of his glory by the Messiah, is extraordinarily wide-spread in the Judaism of the NT period.[6] We have sure knowledge of the belief in a (semi-) divine being 'Man' (Hebrew and Aramaic 'Son of man') that in post-christian times also appears in the Hermes religion, influenced by Egyptian Judaism, in the Naassene hymn and in Manichaeism.[7] Philo seems to have had the idea that in Noah something like a second 'first man' had appeared; and the same may apply to Enoch. The antiquity and origin of the conception of the periodically returning Adam remains doubtful. Nor can the latter be definitely established for the eschatological bringer of salvation which appears in Enoch and IV Ezra.

B. THE 'BODY OF CHRIST'

A precise clarification of the question how far the 'first man'

[1] R. Bultmann, *Gnomon* 26, 1954, p. 183 f.
[2] Quispel, *Eranos-Jahrbuch*, 1953, p. 206 f.
[3] H. Odeberg in *Th.Wh.* II, p. 553 ff., where the parallels between Enoch and Adam are cited.
[4] Test. Levi 18: 'He himself will open the doors of paradise and remove the sword that is threatening Adam;' cf. a great number of other passages in Bousset-Gressmann, *Religion des Judentums*, p. 260 ff.
[5] Yasna 19.30 ff.; cited Staerk, *Soter* II/1, pp. 192 ff., 202.
[6] J. Jeremias, *Th.Wb.* I, p. 142 f.
[7] W. Bousset, *Hauptprobleme der Gnosis*, Göttingen, 1907, p. 181 ff.; the mystery cult of Attis remains very doubtful (p. 183 ff.).

('or king of paradise') includes the whole of mankind or even of the universe, from which conceptions like the Church as the *'body of Christ'* have come, would be instructive.[1]

Before discussing this problem, however, we must mention a very stimulating fact. The same concept of the Church which in the Pauline letters is expressed in terms of 'body of Christ' appears in the images both of the vine (John 15.1 ff.) and of the house or temple (I Peter 2.3 ff.). Both are of Jewish origin (cf. Ps. 80 and *I QS* 8.5–9; 9.3–6).[2] They are combined in the description of Israel in Pseudo-Philo *Antiquitates Biblicae* 12.8–9. And most important of all: Israel is conceived of in these images as pervading the whole cosmos, having its roots in the abyss and its branches near the throne of God. In the same passage the question is raised, whether Israel could be rejected by God in favour of a new-planted vine. This proves that the concept of the Church as 'vine' or as 'temple' is not dependent on a Gnostic saviour-myth, but is rooted in the OT imagery and its development in later Judaism. It is probable that the same is true of the parallel Pauline conception, although the origin of the term 'body of Christ' is more difficult to explain.

Indo-Iranian is the concept of the cosmos as the 'materialization (*Stoffwerdung*) of the deity',[3] or of the 'world-deity' (*Weltengottheit*) whose gigantic body is composed of the elements of the universe.[4] But how old are these Persian authorities? On Greek soil the conception of the world-soul which simultaneously lives at the centre of the cosmos, pervades the whole of it and encompasses it, is a living force from the time of Plato's *Timaeus* (34B, 3–9). In the Stoic philosophy the conception of God as the world-soul acquires central inportance, and the view expressed in the

---

[1] The various hypotheses concerning this question and the scholars who represent them are mentioned in J. A. T. Robinson, *The Body*, London, 1952, p. 55; cf. W. L. Knox, 'Parallels to the NT use of σῶμα', *JThSt*, 39, 1938, pp. 243–246; A. Oepke, 'Leib Christi oder Volk Gottes bei Paulus?' *ThLitZ* 1954, p. 363 ff.; P. Benoit, 'Corps, tête et plérôme dans les épîtres de la captivité,' R. *Biblique* 63, 1956, pp. 5–44; F. Mussner, *Christus, das All und die Kirche*, Trier, 1955, p. 118 ff.

[2] Cf. D. Flusser in *Scripta Hierosolymitana*, IV, 1958, p. 229–236.

[3] A. Jeremias, *Allgemeine Religionsgeschichte*, 1918, p. 6.

[4] G. Bornkamm, *Das Ende des Gesetzes*, München, 1952, p. 142; documentary evidence in R. Reitzenstein, *Studien zum antiken Synkretismus*, I, Stud. Bibl., Warburg, 1926, p. 72 ff.; influence already on Philo: E. Percy, *Der Leib Christi in den paulinischen Homologumena und Antilegomena*, Lund, 1942, p. 50, note 93.

Timaeus that the world is an animated body, maintains itself.[1] God is identical with the *Logos-Pneuma* which pervades the whole of the cosmos and is its soul.[2] The Orphic fragment 21a (preserved in *de mundo* 7, 400B.28 ff.) according to which Zeus is the head and the centre, contains all things within himself and issues all things from himself is also entirely determined by this Stoic idea. Further the same conception appears in a more definite form in Orphic fragment 168, in a Serapis oracle in Macrobius, *Saturnalia* I.20.17 and finally with detailed interpretation regarding the various members in P. Leiden W,[3] in which it is well nigh impossible to make out what is genuinely ancient text.[4] In the Gnostic world-soul such conceptions certainly at least maintain themselves.[5] Widespread in the Greek world, of course, is the identification of the cosmos with God or its descent from God,[6] which finds its continuation in Philo's description of the world as 'God's son.'[7] But all this leads only to the idea that the cosmos, not mankind or even the congregation of the faithful, is the body of the god. Even the idea, long since familiar in the Greek world, of man as a microcosm and the world as a macrocosm which appears again with Philo,[8] or that of the creation of man from all the elements of the cosmos,[9] led only to a relation—god-cosmos-individual. The fact also that at the time of Augustus we can trace the worship of the god Aion (Aeon) who 'in virtue of divine nature ever remains the same and who κατὰ τὰ αὐτά is the one cosmos, as he is and was and will be, having neither beginning nor middle nor end, not subject to any change, effective cause of absolutely eternal nature', or afterwards of the Hermetic Aion who is a second god, mediator between god and the world and who

[1]Festugière, *Hermès*, II, p. 328.
[2]Chrysippus, *Stoic, fr.* II, 1076; cf. also Lev. R.4 (107d): God's relation to the world is like that of the soul to the body (*Str-B.* II, p. 437 f.).
[3]K. Preisendanz, *Papyri Graecae Magicae*, 1928 ff., xiii, 770–2.
[4]Cf. Reitzenstein, *Studien* I, p. 69 ff.
[5]Quispel, *Eranos-Jahrbuch*, 1953, p. 208 ff.; cf. also *Corp. Herm.* XIII.14: 'the body composed of powers'.
[6]Plato, *Tim.* 92c; Diogenes Laertius VII.73; Sextus Emp. adv. math. IX. 95.
[7]*de ebr.* 30; *quod deus immut.* 31.
[8]*quis rer. div. her.* 155, cf. 263; *de migr. Abr.* 220; *de op. mundi* 82.
[9]*de op. mundi* 146; Hellenistic parallels in Festugière, *Hermès* IV, 1954, p. 176 ff.; later Jewish parallels op. cit. I, p. 269, note 2; Quispel *Eranos-Jahrbuch*, 1953, p. 216 f.; Slav. Enoch 30.8.

contains the whole universe within himself,[1]—this certainly shows that the idea of a god who contains the world within himself has widespread influence; but it does not show how mankind is substituted for the cosmos, and this in such a manner that as the community of the saved she belongs together with her Saviour. Stoic parallels of cosmos and human society as a whole would be slightly more closely related.[2]

That such conceptions have also infiltrated into Judaism is shown by the famous passages in Philo where the high priest is equated with the divine Logos, no longer a man, free from sin, mediator,[3] where it is also asserted that 'the older Logos puts on the cosmos as a garment' like the high priest his gown with the heavenly signs. The cosmic symbolism of the high-priestly robe probably originates in ancient Oriental ideas,[4] and these may have persisted, strongly influenced by Stoic ideas, in the speculations on this garment.[5] This may be the origin of the equation cosmos =garment.[6] But even this will not lead us any farther than a relation between the godhead and the cosmos.[7]

We should first of all refer to the Rabbinic sources according to which God is so closely allied to Israel that he shares its whole destiny.[8] Here God also is sent into exile and returns. When he saved Israel he, so to say, saved himself.[9]- This shows at the outset the general idea that, as for the Greeks god and cosmos are tied

[1]Festugière, *Hermès* IV, p. 152 ff.; Hellenistic evidence, p. 176 ff.

[2]Evidence: H. Sasse, *Th.Wb.* III, p. 873 f.; cf. passages like Seneca, *ep. mor.* XIV.4(92) 30; XV.3 (95) 52. Cf. also the references in W. L. Knox, *JThSt*, 39, 1938, pp. 243–6; id. *St Paul and the Church of the Gentiles*, Cambridge, 1925, p. 161 f.; T. A. Lacey, *The one Body and the one Spirit*, London, 1925, p. 54 f. 232.

[3]Especially *de fug. et inv.* 108 ff.; more evidence collected by Schrenk in *Th.Wb.* III, p. 273 f.

[4]H. Ringgren in *ZAW*, 64, 1952, p. 124.

[5]Schrenk, *Th.Wb.* III, p. 274, note 46.

[6]Staerk, *Soter* II/1, p. 181 ff.

[7]*Corp. Herm.* IV.1 does not belong here; for according to XIV.7 not the cosmos but his creative activity must be regarded as the 'body' of God. This conception is foreign to us but also according to Diogenes Laertius VII.38 is πᾶν τὸ ποιοῦν σῶμα; and according to Philo, *somn.* I.30 it had been discussed whether the νοῦς is not σῶμα which Philo indignantly denies.

[8]Dahl, *Das Volk Gottes,* p. 54, cf. p. 224 ff.

[9]The Jewish parallels which are cited by Dr P. Winter in *ThLZ*, 1955, p. 144 f. are very late.

together as a matter of course, so for the Jews are God and
Israel.[1] The quoted parallels (up to *Corpus Hermeticum* XIV.7)
show how obvious, from ancient Oriental or Stoic presupposi-
tions, the concept of the garment or the body of the God was in
order to express a close connexion.

Yet this by itself would not be a sufficient explanation. That
Adam, as the father of the race, determined the whole destiny of
the succeeding generation was a widespread Jewish view.[2] When
Philo calls Noah the 'progenitor of the new human race' (*de
Abramo* 46; similarly *Vit. Mos.* II.60, 65; *Quaest. in Gen.* 1.96) then
this shows not only that the ancient idea of the father of the race
still influences him but also that he too regards Noah as the second
Adam. Adam however is the most suitable character because he,
though originally regarded as the father of a tribe, became more
and more a mythical figure. A Hellenist does not think in the
'horizontal', temporal context, but in the vertical, local sense. He
must say that all men are 'included in Adam'. And the more
'Adam' becomes a purely mythical figure and loses his historical
character, the more obvious are assertions like that of Adam as
the '*guf*', the container of all succeeding souls.[3] *Syriac Baruch* 23.4
states only that at the time of Adam's fall all those who were yet
to be born, already numbered, were kept in an appointed place,
but it clearly shows the transition from temporal to local thinking.[4] Thus the ideas are already there. The Church adopts them
to express the knowledge that Jesus has fulfilled Israel's way and
is therefore the Representative of the new Israel. His crucified
and risen body is always present for the believer who shares in
his blessings and lives under his lordship.[5] That the title 'Son of
man' is particularly suitable to express the idea of the Church

[1] Cf. p. 47, n. 1.
[2] E.g. IV Ezra 3.7, 21 f.; 7.118; Syr. Bar. 17.3; 23.4; 48.42; 54.15, 19. For
the identification of Adam with the patriarch Jacob–Israel and with the divine
logos cf. p. 46.
[3] Which appears for the first time in Patristic literature, Staerk, *Soter* II/1,
p. 125 ff.; all the other evidence is either uncertain or late. Cf. G. Scholem,
Eranos-Jahrbuch 22, 1953, p. 239 f.
[4] IV Ezra 4.41 does not belong here (in spite of what H. Gunkel says in
E. Kautzsch, *Die Apokryphen und Pseudepigraphen des alten Testaments*,
Tübingen, 1900, p. 358, note d, this is not referring to the pre-existent souls).
Cf. also Dahl, *Volk Gottes,* p. 114 f.; W. D. Davies, *Paul and Rabbinic Judaism,*
Manchester, 1916, p. 57.
[5] Cf. p. 47 f.

belonging to him, also makes the adoption of the Adam theory easier. It is not accidental that Paul places the ἐν χριστῷ parallel to ἐν Ἀδάμ, assuming as a matter of course that Christ is *the* '(Son of) Man'.[1] If we recall further what was said in connexion with the story of the temptation, then it should be clear that Paul regards the intimate unity of the Church with Christ (Rom. 5.12 ff.; 6.1 ff.) very much from the point of view of those Adam ideas, and that he is already drawing on tradition.[2] Perhaps Adam had already become a clearly mythical character to pre-Christian (Hellenistic) Judaism,[3] 'containing within himself' all generations.[4] Then the 'local' pattern of thought would already have been substituted for the 'temporal' pattern, and have led to the conception that the whole of mankind with its destiny was included 'in him'='in his body'.[5] The relation of the beginning (*Urzeit*) with the last days (*Endzeit*) may then have led people to regard the '(Son of) Man', Jesus, as the restored, the second 'Man', the 'last' Adam (1 Cor. 15.45, 47).[6] The idea would thus have arisen from Adam's fall. There would have been no pre-Christian reference to the saviour who had already appeared. But the expectation of the eschatological '(Son of) Man' would have to lead to his equation with the second Adam. Paul knows that this One has already come.

Whether and through which channels the Indo-Iranian conception of the world as the body of the god, or the Jewish conception of the souls which live in Adam as their 'container', had any influence as early as the days of the NT is a matter of mere conjecture. In second century Gnosticism the pre-historic saviour appears and this is contrary to the Iranian scheme as it certainly is to the NT. This identification with the sum total of the divine sparks of all the souls is neither Iranian—there one can say at the utmost that the human race has descended from him—nor indeed

[1] I Cor. 15.22, 27, where Ps. 8 is applied to Jesus as if this were a matter of course; but also ὁ εἷς ἄνθρωπος Ἰησοῦς Χριστός Rom. 5.15!

[2] Cf. also E. Best, *One Body*, pp. 34–43, 83–95, 215–225 and p. 45 ff. here.

[3] Cf. e.g. *Vita Ad.* 47; *Apoc. Mos.* 39.

[4] Cf. the evidence of the 'cosmic Adam' in Staerk, *Soter* II/1, p. 15 ff., belonging to a later period; also Metatron, op. cit., p. 115.

[5] The corporate meaning of 'body' (in English; for the Greek cf. the author's article σῶμα in *Th.Wb.*) has scarely influenced Paul (N. Clark, *Approach*, p. 66).

[6] Cf. the conception of the 'first Adam' in IV Ezra 3.21.

in accordance with the NT. The conception of a saviour who saves himself is absent from both.[1]

C.   ON THE QUESTION OF THE ORIGIN OF GNOSTICISM

After the publication of the newly discovered Gnostic texts[2] the inquiry into this question can perhaps be carried farther, but at present we can say no more than the following. The so-called 'Gnostic' experience of the world is undoubtedly to be found in *Hellenism*: the dread of existence, the feeling of being closed in, the longing for heaven; also the conception of the origin of the soul from heaven and its return there. This can be conceived as the *Logos* or *Nous* being changed into the soul or as settling in it. In the latter case 'the divine' cannot only, as the *Nous*, dwell in the soul but, as the divine element, it can be distinguished from 'soul and body' as the human element, as is the case with the *Pneuma* of later Gnosticism.[3] The *Logos* or *Nous* also often appears personified and identified with traditional deities. Here the categories of singularity and plurality appear, inasmuch as the souls are disseminated from the sun and will return to it again. One will remember the *Logos spermatikos* and Plutarch's interpretation of the Osiris and Dionysos Zagreus myth as referring to the *Logos* (*de Is. et Os.* 53 f., p. 372 F ff.). On the other hand the ancient Gnostic work published by C. Schmidt[4] identifies the collection of the members of the *Logos* with the collection of the dispersed Israelites. In all these cases it may be true that the knowledge of this origin of the soul has saving efficacy; but the figure of a saviour is lacking or at best reduced to a symbol of the soul's destiny. The mystery religions certainly do have other saviour-figures, in whose destiny the mystic perhaps participates, but no descent from heaven is attributed to them.

On the other hand in the near *Orient*, in *Judaism*, for example,

[1]Cf. W. Manson, *Jesus the Messiah*, p. 246, 255.
[2]An edition of photographic plates of the manuscripts is now being issued: Antiquities Department. Coptic Gnostic Papyri in the Coptic Museum of Old Cairo. Dr Pahor Labib, Vol. I, Cairo 1956, Government Press. *The Gospel according to Thomas* is published by A. Guillaumont and others, Leiden, New York, 1959.
[3]Xenocrates according to Plutarch, *de Is. et Os.* 360E, and on this *ThZ*, 1953, p. 76 f.
[4]*Koptisch-gnostische Schriften* (= *Griech. christl. Schriftsteller* 13.1), pp. 350, 35 f.

we find the figure of the 'first man', or the king of paradise called 'Man', and at least in Enoch and IV Ezra the expectation of the Messiah-'Man' according to the scheme of 'latter days' corresponding with the 'first days'. But outside the NT there is no reference to a saviour who has already come in this context. It is true that Haenchen[1] demonstrates the probability that the statement that Simon Magus was the 'great power of God' (Acts 8.9 f.) is pre-Christian while his description as a 'sorcerer' might be a Christian distortion; but G. Kretschmar[2] has shown correctly that all that can be ascertained historically with any certainty is in fact only the assertion of a Samaritan *Goet* that he was a revelation of God. But this only leads to that Judaism in which Messianic figures also appeared (Mark 13.22; Acts 5.36 f.). If one recognizes that all the Gnostic systems known to date seem to draw at least *also* on a syncretistic Judaism,[3] then one will have to ask if, on the one hand, Hellenistic myths of the descent and ascent of the soul did not amalgamate with the Oriental concept of the 'first man' in order to represent the pre-historic fall of the divine into matter, while, on the other hand, Jewish expectations of the Messiah led to the figure of the saviour. The stories of Adam in Genesis have been decisive for the first amalgamation.[4] *Adam* is probably the one who is speaking in the so-called 'Mithras-liturgy'.[5] *He* is the one who calls for deliverance from Ἀνάγκη and εἱμαρμένη, the δαίμων ἀέριος. Cf. Appendices A and B.

Then one would have to ask if the assertion that the saviour had already come, in so far as this is not merely a symbol of the pre-historic descent of the divine soul-power into matter, is not a statement meant to compete with the Christian message that the 'Man' who was to come at the end of time was present in Jesus of Nazareth. The Qumran texts, it is true, show a pronounced

---

[1] E. Haenchen, *ZThK*, 1952, 336 ff.

[2] G. Kretschmar, *EvTh*, 1953, p. 358.

[3] G. Kretschmar, *EvTh*, 1953, p. 360; cf. C. H. Dodd, *The Bible and the Greeks*, London, 1935, p. 99; Quispel, Eranos-Jahrbuch, 1953, p. 195 ff; the reference to Gen. 6.1 ff. in H. J. Schoeps. *ZRGG*, 1954, p. 278 is not sufficient. Contrary to this view: H. J. Schoeps. *ThLZ*, 1956, p. 420 f.

[4] Quispel, *Eranos-Jahrbuch*, 1953, p. 202 ff.; probably confirmed by the new discoveries: *ZRGG*, 1954, p. 302 ff.

[5] E. Peterson, R. *Biblique*, 1948, p. 201 f.

dualism,[1] 'Gnostic' contrasting ideas like 'Light/Darkness' and also a strong emphasis on the 'knowledge' of God,[2] but the figure of a saviour only in the sense of a '*teacher* of righteousness'.[3] The 'model' that Quispel[4] draws of the oldest Jewish Gnosticism knows of no saviour and of no 'first man'. 'If there may perhaps have been a pre-Christian Gnosis, there has never been a pre-Christian saviour.' Thus Gnosticism was certainly not merely Hellenized Christianity, as A. von Harnack thought; but the question does arise if Christian missionary preaching, indirectly through syncretistic Judaism, has not given the impulse to the welding together of already existing elements into a myth proper and above all into a saviour-religion.

[1] This dualism, it is true, is primarily ethical, but it also encroaches on the physical sphere, W. Baumgartner, *Schw. Theol. Umschau*, 1954, p. 62, in contrast to K. G. Kuhn, *ZThK*, 1952, p. 296 ff.; also K. Schubert, *ThLZ*, 1953, p. 498.

[2] On the distinction from Gnosticism cf. W. D. Davies, *Harvard ThR*, 1953, p. 131 ff.; K. Schubert, *ThLZ*, 1953, p. 502 ff.; Bo Reicke, *NTSt* I, 1954–5, p. 137 ff.; M. Burrows, *The Dead Sea Scrolls*, New York, 1955, p. 253 ff.; F. Nötscher, *Zur theologischen Terminologie der Qumrantexte*, Bonn, 1956, register; R. McL. Wilson, *The Gnostic Problem*, London, 1958, p. 73 ff., also 225 ff. Regarding the whole problem cf. recently H. Jonas, *The Gnostic Religion*, Boston, 1958; R. M. Grant, *Gnosticism and Early Christianity*, New York, 1959; for Qumran cf. F. M. Cross, *The Ancient Library of Qumran and Modern Biblical Studies*, New York, 1958; U. Wilckens, *Weisheit und Torheit*, Tübingen, 1959.

[3] G. Molin, *Die Söhne des Lichtes*, 1954, p. 147 f.

[4] *Eranos-Jahrbuch*. 1953, pp. 201 f., 224; also *ThLZ*, 1956, p. 686.

INDEX OF BIBLICAL REFERENCES

Index of Biblical References

Bible Ref.	Page
Acts	
3.21	58
4.10	58, 95
4.24 ff.	58
4.25	50, 58
4.27	50
4.30	50
5.30	58
5.30 f.	95
5.31	38, 58, 74, 94
5.32	58, 66
5.35	58
5.36 f.	126
7.32	33
7.55 f.	38
7.56	40, 41, 57
8.9 f.	126
8.32 f.	50
9.4 f.	99
9.14	56
10.38	33
10.39 f.	58
10.40	95
10.41	66, 95
10.42	37, 95
10.43	58, 94
11.27	22
13.17–25	58
13.27	58
13.27–29	58
13.29 f.	58
13.30	95
13.31	66
13.33	36, 43, 73
13.33 f.	95
13.38	94
14.15	58
14.15–17	95
15.4	33
15.7	28
15.12	33
17.3	95
17.22–31	95
17.24	58
17.30	58
17.31	37
21.9–11	22
22.7 f.	99
22.14	33
22.16	56

Bible Ref.	Page
Acts	
24.26	39
26.14 f.	99
26.20	58
Romans	
1.3 f.	51, 56, 58, 59, 64, 67, 95
1.4	37, 43, 63, 73
3.4	65
3.25	52
4.25	50
5.12	54
5.12 ff.	46, 54, 124
5.15	124
5.19	75
6.1 ff.	124
6.4 f.	111
7.4	111
8.3	113
8.32	50
8.34	50, 74, 75
8.36	91
8.38 f.	75, 110
9.6 ff.	46, 82
10.6	102
10.9	75
10.16	50
11.33 ff.	61
14.9	75
15.21	50
I Corinthians	
1.2	56
2.2	53
6.2	26
8.4–6	95
8.6	75, 95, 102, 110
10.4	102
10.16	111
10.17	111
11.23	34, 95
11.23 ff.	50, 52
11.24	103, 111
11.27	111
11.29	111
12.3	75
ch. 13	61
15.3	65, 95, 114
15.3 f.	114
15.3–5	52, 66, 114, 115

Bible Ref.	Page
I Corinthians	
15.4	95, 114
15.5 f.	38
15.6	52
15.21 ff.	46
15.22	54, 124
15.25 f.	75
15.27	124
15.31	91
15.34	100
15.45	46, 124
15.47	124
16.22	56
II Corinthians	
1.4–7	91
4.10	91
4.11	50
4.12	91
4.14	48
4.15	91
5.14	111
5.14 f.	55
5.18 f.	66
6.3–10	91
7.3	48
8.9	75, 102, 113
12.2	40
12.2 ff.	57
Galatians	
1.16	57
2.19	113
3.13	53, 113
3.16	48
3.28	48
3.29	48
4.3	109
4.4	102, 113
4.8	75
4.8–10	109
4.25 f.	60
6.14	53
6.16	47
6.17	47, 91
Ephesians	
1.20	74
2.16	111
4.5	47
5.14	94

Index of Biblical References